DIOCLETIAN

THE TALE OF A SINGULAR MAN

DIOCLETIAN
THE TALE OF A SINGULAR MAN

a novel in verse by
Adrian Higham

with illustrations by
Christopher Aggs

WRP

WHYKE ROAD PRESS

First published 1995

Copyright © Adrian Higham 1995

The right of Adrian Higham to be identified as the Author of this Work has been asserted in accordance with the Copyright, Design & Patents Act 1988.

All rights reserved. No part of this book may be reproduced or utilized in any form or by any means, electronic or mechanical, including photocopying, recording or by information storage and retrieval system, without permission in writing from the Publisher.

British Library Cataloguing in Publication Data
A catalogue record for this book is available from the British Library.

ISBN   0 9526291 0 0

Published by: Whyke Road Press, 17 Whyke Road, Chichester,
                  West Sussex, PO19 2HN, England
                  Phone (01243) 783930   Fax (01243) 773273

Printed in Great Britain by Villiers Publications Ltd., London, N3 2LE

Typeset by John Carden, 7 Cleveland Road, Chichester, PO19 2HF

A Singular Man

This, my friends, is the tale of a singular man,
Who saved his world when others tried and failed.
He re-established Roman imperial power
That it might last another thousand years.

Know that the city of Rome, already old,
Had proudly passed its own millennium
When Diocletian spent his boyhood years
At Salona by the Adriatic sea.
Humbly born, he grew to rule the world
And then held sway for more than twenty years
Until he chose to leave of his own free will.

But in the seventy years before he ruled
A score of emperors fleetingly held power
Trying to keep the imperial frontiers safe
Against the innumerable barbarian hordes.
Within the Empire all was disarray,
The land untilled, good men in short supply,
Commerce undone, the gods themselves asleep –

And into this world there came this singular man…

CONTENTS

THE WORLD OF DIOCLETIAN, A MAP	viii
BACKGROUND AND BEGINNINGS	1
LEARNING THE TRADE	11
AURELIAN THE EXAMPLE	17
ZENOBIA	27
PREPARATION	39
THE PERSIAN CAMPAIGN: OPPORTUNITY	65
TO HAVE AND TO HOLD	81
FULFILLING THE DREAM	103
THE EXERCISE OF AUTHORITY	117
SO MUCH TO DO	133
THE NEED TO SHARE THE LOAD	147
PROBLEMS ABOUND	157
THE PERSIAN THREAT	165
THE GREAT VICTORY	177
AGAINST INFLATION	189
AGAINST THE CHRISTIANS	199
THE TRIUMPH AND THE SHADOW	225
REDUCED TO THIS	235
THE LAST CHAPTER	245
SOURCES AND REFERENCES	260

TUNGRIA
• Mainz
R. Rhine
R. Danube
RAETIA
Carnuntum •
Arrabona •
PANNONIA
• Milan
Sirmium • • Viminacium
• Arles
• Ravenna
R. Danube
Salona
MOESIA
• Rome
• Lychnidus
• Tebessa

0 — 500kms
300mls

THE WORLD OF DIOCLETIAN

ostorum

Nicomedia

BITHYNIA **CAPPADOCIA**

dyma

Tyana   Nisibis

R. Tigris

R. Euphrates

Antioch

Emesa Palmyra

Ctesiphon

Tyre

Alexandria

DMS

BACKGROUND AND BEGINNINGS
in which the scene is set

The Oracle

    The stench of burning homesteads lingered on,
    As the old man slowly climbed the valley side,
    The evening glow was fading into night.
    He sought the oracle. He had to know
    What would become of all he knew and loved.
    Would the chaos of the present ever pass?

Drowned in the depths of despair you must wonder
                          if you will recover.
Into your world be assured there will come
                          such a man who can save you.
Only be quick to obey without question
                          and follow no other,
Carefully listen to him and eschew all those faults
                          you are slave to.
Look, he will come and straightway be ready
                          to selflessly serve you.
End now your doubts, for the time is at hand
                          and these are the portents:
There will be disasters and wars, and the plague,
                          hidden deaths in high places;
Into this chaos will come with authority
                          one whose importance
All will acclaim as he strikes down the boar
                          and removes all the traces.
None of your doubts or despair will remain;
                          this man will preserve you.

DIOCLETIAN

A Mother's Prayer

SALONA
AD 245
aet. 2

Soundly sleep dear son of mine
Soundly sleep, soundly sleep.
Safely keep Great Powers divine
This son of mine, safely keep.
Banish all that is malign
From my son – him safely keep.

Help me Gods to help my boy
Safely into manhood grow.
May good fortune he enjoy,
Authority and power know.
May he all those gifts employ
Which you dear Gods on him bestow.

— ✽ —

He stirs. What dreams he of? What frightening beast?
The roaring lion, the ape, the fierce wild boar?
This miniature man, perfectly made, is mine
And yet he is alone, distinct from me.
His thoughts, his dreams, are his. I am apart.
Every day he grows away from me
But nonetheless, part of me is there.
Where'er he goes I will go with him,
Whatever the road, however the journey ends.

Now he awakes and we must back to work.
His father, showing his love, sent him this book
Which he wrote himself with utmost care,
And had a friend draw all the animals.
He sent precise instructions that our boy
Should read and learn a letter every day
That he might hear him read when he next came
To visit us at Salona. I too must learn
The letters and the rhymes to help our son.
So back to work – I know where he will start,
The wild boar, Aper, with its fearsome gaze
As if by magic draws the boy to him.
So back to work – the longest road begins
With the first step – A is for Aper the boar.

Alphabet

A   **is for Aper**. Aper the boar.
      It is as wild a beast as ever you saw.

B   **is for Bos**. Bos is the ox.
      It pulls a big cart, full up with rocks.

C   **is for Canis**. Canis the dog.
      It will sleep in the house or under a log.

D   **is Delphinus**. That is a dolphin.
      Its movement is smooth and so is its skin.

E   **is for Equus**. Equus the horse.
      It is of great power, also of great force.

F   **is for Feles**. Feles the cat.
      It will sleep by the fire or sit on the mat.

G   **is for Glis**. The little dormouse.
      So tiny that it gets lost in the house.

H   **is for Hinnus**. Hinnus the mule.
      It pulls a great load. It can take you to school.

I   **is for Ibis**. Ibis the bird.
      This is holy in Egypt so I have heard.

L   **is for Leo**. Leo the lion.
      He is the king which you must keep an eye on.

M   **is for Melis**. Melis the badger.
      He is a night scavenger and he is a cadger.

N   **is for Nepa**. Nepa the scorpion.
      Beware of its tail and of its poison.

DIOCLETIAN

O **is for Ovis.** Ovis the sheep.
These you must count to go to sleep.

P **is Papilio.** It is the butterfly.
Both lovely at rest and in the bright sky.

Q [A lacuna in the manuscript at this point]

R **is for Rana.** Rana the frog.
It croaks in fine weather and in the fog.

S **is for Simia.** Simia the ape.
It is almost like us, not quite the same shape.

T **is for Turtur.** Turtur the turtledove.
Its name is like its call in the great tree above.

U **is for Ursus.** Ursus the bear.
When roused he gets angry, he is someone to fear.

V **is for Vulpes.** Vulpes the fox.
He hides in the scrubland among all the rocks.

X **is for Xiphias.** That is a swordfish.
And that is the one with which we will finish.

Z [lacuna]

What's in a name?

When Diocletian was a boy,
He had a humbler name.
He was called Diocles,
Before he came to fame.

Dí-öc-lēs is hard to scan
Because of the diphthong.
Either you can say Díe-clēs,
Or Dí-öc-lēs, for neither's wrong.

When Dí-öc-lēs achieved his goal
And was Emperor,
Maximian and he swapped names,
Then Díe-clēs had four.

BACKGROUND AND BEGINNINGS

Gaius Valerius, he had from birth,
From Maximian, Aurelius,
And Dí-öc-lēs was made to be
As Diocletian all glorious.

When Diocletian abdicated
At the ending of his reign,
He showed he knew what's in a name,
By becoming Díe-clēs once again.

A Father's Concern AD 261
aet. 17

"Pass the wine, good sir, I trust it's to your taste?
my friend the steward recommended it
as suitable for this time of day."

"Indeed, it's excellent, Master Scribe,
as you would expect from the cellar of a senator.
But tell me why the honour of this pleasant drink
sitting here on the terrace as the sun goes down?"

"I find it good to pass the time of day with friends –
but doubly good to gain good counsel too.
Frankly sir, I need advice about my boy.
You know, he lives with his mother down in Salona,
and she worries me what is to become of him."

"Worry about your son, but that's absurd!
You've done well with Senator Anullinus,
you are now free and high in his regard."

"Indeed, that's true, but for Gaius I want more.
You've been a soldier. You have seen the world.
What can I do to start him well
so he can rise to do great things
and be remembered when I am long forgot?"

"It's true, the world's an uncertain place.
When we were young, all seemed calm and clear
but now the masters come and go;
the armies formed and reformed –
generals up and generals down –
barbarians from the north – revolts abound.
Uncertainty breeds uncertain certainty."

DIOCLETIAN

"My friend, you wax lyrical about our sad affairs.
But what to do – I have a son to place."

"Allow me my say. I will be practical.
These uncertain times do have one certain thread.
Opportunities lie in Fortune's rapid change.
Many young soldiers become great overlords
and Illyria's tough young men are without compare.

Let your son become a legionary.
He will do well in the army, I am sure,
and in due course join the Protector corps.
They are in demand, these keen young officers,
being on call for all the senior staff.
There are some who serve the Emperor personally.

Tomorrow let me speak to my friend Lucius.
I am sure he will write a letter of commendation.
Now where is that wine? The steward indeed was right,
It makes the best of company as the sun goes down!"

Generals up, and Generals down!

211 AD	Ab Urbe Condita 964
	Septimus Severus was no more;
	An exceptional happening, it must be said,
	The emperor actually died in bed!
	Caracalla and **Geta** then succeeded.
	Caracalla killed Geta; he wasn't needed;
	They started as joint emperors,
	And alone he ruled for six more years –
	His Praetorian Prefect murdered him
	Which the Army thought distinctly dim
217 AD	For this **Macrinus** made such economies
218 AD	That when **Elagabalus** claimed the purple his,
	The Army agreed and Macrinus was killed.
	Now Elagabalus' time with Baal was filled
	As Priest, but being of the Severan line,
	All seemed for him and his grandma fine

BACKGROUND AND BEGINNINGS

        Till he took his god, which was a black rock,
            To imperial Rome; this caused a shock.
        It gave his grandma such concern
222 AD   That she said it's **Severus Alexander's** turn.

        Now Severus' mother was number one
            And ruled the empire through her son.
        In east and west war was the course;
            Making the emperor divide his force.

        Thirteen years on, he tries to buy peace.
            "To give money to Germans. The practice must cease."
        So said the Army camped by the Rhine,
            Killed him and his mother, and ended the line.

235 AD   The Army elected **Maximin Thrax**,
            But he drove his men whom he thought lax
        Which made them think that others would,
            On the imperial throne, be just as good.

        So Thrax was killed at Aquillea
            Then four men tried, it cost them dear,
        Seizing the purple as chance arises
238 AD   Precipitating the year of crises.

239 AD   Then **Gordian 3**, a mere lad of thirteen
            Lasted five years and for help he was seen
        To depend upon others, becoming their tools,
            Some they were able but others were fools.

244 AD   Then **Philip the Arabian**, the last of these
            Said "Enough", came to Rome, the purple to seize.
        An outsider ruled Rome at the millennium,
            Which shows to what a pass its fortunes had come.

        But north of the Danube the Goths caused a problem
            So Philip sent Decius to Dacia to stop them.
        There the purple he took as if was his right
249 AD   So **Decius** then had Philip to fight.

        Philip is killed in the civil war
            But the Goths in Dacia rise once more.
        Briefly Decius controlled it all
            Then Decius and his legions fall.

DIOCLETIAN

251 AD	First two generals stake their claim
253 AD	Then from the Rhine, **Valerian** came,
	Ending thus the civil war
	Re-establishing the rule of law.

    Valerian then attacks the Persians
        With a different conclusion to previous excursions,
    For he is defeated and made a forced guest,
        Then put to death at Sapor's behest.

260 AD	**Gallienus**, his son, now rules alone
	But there is not much he can call his own
	For the Goths and the Alemanni find
	They are free to roam all unconfined.

    Gallienus held Italy, that was all.
        A Roman usurper ruled in Gaul;
    With Sapor triumphant in the east,
        The plague destroyed both great and least.

    He fought back with vigour, remade his forces,
        Speedily reacting with soldiers on horses.
    The Alemanni, he forced to flee
        And regained from the Goths control of the sea.

    But then his headquarters made a coup
        And thus the Illyrians broke through.
    These tough new Romans took command
        And drove the barbarians from the land.

268 AD	First came **Claudius** who conquered the Goth,
	Then came **Aurelian**, all feared his wrath,
	Fiercely campaigning, dubbed "sword in hand",
	Was by his bodyguard at last unmanned.
275 AD	Two tried briefly I have to relate
	It is required to keep the record straight.
276 AD	Then it was **Probus** as choice of the Army.
	But he made them dig which they thought balmy.
	They caught him alone at the top of a tower
282 AD	So then it was **Carus** who came to power.
	In the Persian realm he pushed his luck,
	They say by lightning he was struck.

BACKGROUND AND BEGINNINGS

283 AD
    His son **Numerian** in a litter
        Was carried home as he was not fitter
    And secretly in it he was killed.
284 AD
        His place was by **Diocletian** filled.

    Emperors then, more than a score,
        In seventy years, had come to the fore,
    Then Diocletian reversed the trend –
        Ruled twenty years, and that is the end!

The End of the Beginning

AD 262
aet. 18

Young men of Salona, have you heard the news?
The recruiting officer has come at last.
Make haste to the office for the interviews
As the quota is being used up fast.

Bring your letters of commendation.
Prepare to answer all their queries.
There will be a detailed examination
To find out about you all that there is.

They will want to know that you are free,
No slave may serve in the legions of Rome.
They will demand from you a guarantee
That you have no civic duties at home.

They will measure you to ensure
You are five foot ten inches tall,
But if they need rather more
They will take an average overall.

They will check your age because they need
Men of eighteen to twenty-five.
They are seeking some who can read
And some who in rough country thrive.

And when the interviews are done,
The military oath everyone will take
To serve wherever Rome's writ may run
And the legions' Eagles never forsake.

DIOCLETIAN

Now is the time you have waited for;
They will distribute the viaticum,
The joining money, which you will draw;
Three gold aurei is a tidy sum.

You will join the draft and march away
To the legion on the frontier in the north.
You will get the mark on a later day,
When you have proved your soldier's worth.

The long awaited time is here,
Your army life can now begin.
Grow in the service, year by year,
And many glorious honours win.

LEARNING THE TRADE
in which Diocles grows in military competence

The Recruit ARRABONA
AD 262
aet. 18

"Well. Let's 'ave yer!", or words to that effect,
Greeted the draft, who didn't know what to expect.
They had been together for a month or more,
Had often talked of what might be in store,
And with what challenges they must contend
When finally they reached their journey's end.
Here was the first, this roaring giant of a man.
With this greeting their legionary life began.

"Get fell in! And number by the right!"
Gradually the men overcame their initial fright
And grasped the meaning of this Titan's roar
Somehow they made a line – one, two, three, four…
Each man numbered, and so the lot was cast
With whom their time of training would be passed;
For next some lesser Titans began to shout
"All those with numbers 'one' fall out on me!"
And then another "numbers 'two' on me."
When eleven, twelve, etc. understood
That they with one, and two, etc. should
Combine together, so the draft was split
In smaller groups that in a tent might fit.

"Now what have the gods, this time, presented me
To make me happy. Stand still. Let me see!"

DIOCLETIAN

The lesser Titan looked at his motley crew –
Three country lads, a smith with eyes askew,
A small dark man who might have been a thief,
Two giggling youths who promised only grief,
And then one standing quietly there apart,
Whose very stance did confidence impart,
Not overweening, but considering
What every new experience might bring.

"Now pay attention! Stop that giggling there.
[How those two cheated the system is not clear.
By choosing all the ones, then twos, we should
Divide the old civilian groups for good.]
The eight of you will now be in my power
Throughout the next four months for every hour.
I am your decanus; to me you will defer.
My name's Marius but you will call me 'sir'.

All of you will mess together, sleep together,
Work together, and you'll learn together.
The Tenth Legion Gemina is now your home,
The finest legion of imperial Rome;
As new recruits you've joined the ninth cohort,
And in the second century the gods have brought
You lucky lads, to this the smartest tent,
And that it so remains is my intent."

Diocles listened and he looked around:
The youths were nervously staring at the ground,
The small dark man absorbing what he heard
To take advantage of all as it occurred,
The country lads just grinned – they always did,
For thoughts they hardly had and hardly hid,
Open faced, strong as the beasts they tended,
But hard to tell how much they comprehended,
As hard to know just what the big smith knew,
Scowling, arms akimbo, eyes askew.

Diocles, with this group, must learn the trade
Of soldiering, the use of pick and spade,
Of marching mile on mile, of carrying loads,
Of digging ditches, breaking stone for roads,

LEARNING THE TRADE

Of fighting in defence and in attack,
And above all else, of carrying on his back
His weapons, entrenching tool, his kit and stores,
So Rome may triumph in her many wars.

Going to War AD 271
aet. 27

My lord Aurelian's going to war,
    He's conquered many but seeking more.
The army needs to be increased
    To fight Zenobia in the East.

My lord Aurelian's going to war,
    On the Danube legions he will draw
So sufficient troops he'll have to hand
    To enforce his rule throughout the land.

My lord Aurelian's going to war,
    Once more they'll hold Rome's name in awe.
The call's gone out both far and wide;
    The Emperor's word won't be denied.

Send only your bravest and your best
    To take part in this noble quest.
Of honour and fame you can be sure
    For My lord Aurelian's going to war.

— ✽ —

The legionary commander was worried; he was worried sick.
He had to send a detachment, but whom should he pick?
The field army of the Emperor Aurelian was moving east;
He was drawing on the legions that his army might be increased.
The commander had returned to Arrabona only yesterday
To find the imperial orders. He dare not delay.

He turned to his colleagues: "They are calling for a thousand men,
But if we send that many, what will the position be then?
The Legion is short as it is. Will the barbarians stay quiet?
They will attack when they hear we are short; you can be sure they will try it."

The Senior Tribune interrupted, before he could carry on:
"Why not consult Primuspilus, as senior centurion
His experience is vast; he will know how many will suffice."

DIOCLETIAN

The Primuspilus was called and asked for his considered advice.
He thought for a moment. (He had been in this position before,
Numerous were the times he had been asked by his chief to restore
Difficult situations aggravated by decisions not taken.)
"This, Sir, is hardly a problem, if I am not mistaken.
We should send some beginners and some experienced men
They should provide an example and make a strong unit then.
The strongest cohort is the third, and the ninth I suggest
As that has the best trainees, and I'll list the rest
That will be required for the administration and specialists.
If you agree, I'll suggest suitable names and prepare you the lists."

"Excellent, Primuspilus. Do that as soon as you can."
The Legionary Commander felt good; he had produced a sound plan!

The honour of the Legion depended as so often it did
On the Primuspilus getting his colleagues to do what he bid.
He summoned the senior centurions of the ninth and the third,
Reviewed their nominal role, asked whom they preferred
From the other cohorts to fully bring theirs up to strength,
Considered the specialists needed so they achieved at length
Sufficient surveyors, advancemen, blacksmiths and clerks
And cavalry, all listed and named with appropriate remarks.
They checked the waggons and mules enough for each section;
They inspected the various stores awaiting collection.

They carefully considered the tribunes who might be commanding,
For responsibilities of being on detachment are extremely demanding,
And how to persuade their commander to accept their view,
For the wrong choice at this level could all their good work undo.
Finally by the end of the day the choice had been made
Of the thousand men that the imperial order be obeyed.

And what of Diocles in all this bustle and rush
His name was included on the lists; he was there in the crush.

"You are short of a centurion in the ninth, I believe, my friend."

"That's so Primuspilus, but who do you suggest we send?"

"There is that Diocles recently promoted, he's sound,
He's a careful thinking man. He'll learn a lot – that I'll be bound.
He'll go far – it's my private opinion and that's for just us."

So was launched the career of Diocles to be Caesar Augustus.

LEARNING THE TRADE

The Quartermaster's Advice   AD 271
aet. 27

"Be sure, my lad, you keep your records straight."
The Quartermaster stretched – scratched his back and said:
"…and good intelligence – d'you think it's just by chance
that I have these stores and no one has to wait?
D'you think I can keep everybody fed
with all this food only by happenstance?

Records and good intelligence – you've a lot to learn.
This detachment, for you, is a great experience."
The Quartermaster paused and then went on like this:
"To survive Great Rome must to its armies turn –
but armies which starve are hardly the best defence.
Between what they need and can get, there's a great abyss.

We've records and forms to allocate fairly what's there.
No one without proper forms can legally obtain
all that's needed to preserve the Empire of Rome
for without legal form all would be chaos and fear.
And to ensure you've enough, your intelligence network maintain
so what's yours by right ends up real close to home!

I know the Stores Superintendent on the Governor's staff –
he sees we get our fair share of food and wine.
I keep thoroughly informed of developments everywhere
so on getting our orders, there was no need to cut rations in half.
There is enough here to make sure these boys of mine
are fully equipped and provided – with some to spare.

Be sure you've warrants for sufficient further stores –
You've twenty days' but the march'll take a longer time.
Make sure your advancemen go regularly ahead to reserve
all you'll require and make sure it's legally yours
for seizing supplies without legal form is a crime
even for the Army which has the whole world to preserve."

The Lesson   CAPPADOCIA
AD 271
aet. 27

   The highland road's a dusty road
      With peasants working in the fields
   Watching the soldiers marching past
      Dust covers all, armour and shields.

DIOCLETIAN

The road from Ancyra towards the south east
    Is a military road from time out of mind.
While armies come and the armies go
    The peasants continue the perpetual grind.

The army before Tyana is held,
    The city below the Cilician Gates,
The Emperor requires to be reinforced;
    His fury increases the longer he waits.

Now find the detachment from Gemina Ten
    Force-marching through the stifling dust;
In the vanguard, Diocles all alert
    Notes the peasants' bleak distrust.

Asking the scouts the reason for this,
    The rebellious feeling everywhere,
He hears that units in the line ahead
    Have seized the crops when none's to spare.

The Fifth Macedonian up the line
    Had faced a riot and they'd lost men,
Delaying the column at this critical time
    In the campaign of the Emperor Aurelian.

Diocles considered the moral of this,
    The quartermaster's sound advice –
"Good intelligence and due legal form" –
    For everything a proper price.

AURELIAN THE EXAMPLE
in which Diocles first observes the exercise of imperial power

The Fall of Tyana AD 271
aet. 27

Release your imagination, all is there –
The citizens of Tyana, filled with fear,
The Roman army circled all around.
Now look more closely at the further ground –
The road to the Orient climbing up the Taurus,
The busy rush of war lies there before us.
The great Aurelian's progress till this hour
Had been maintained through his tremendous power.
The cities of Asia all had welcomed him
Opened their gates, fearing for life and limb.

The Queen Zenobia has for years held sway,
From Hellespont to Egypt, all her obey.
From far Palmyra in the desert sands
This noble Queen despatches her commands
Throughout the East, so people now neglect
The rule of Rome, which has utterly lost respect.

The Emperor Aurelian, a mighty man of war,
Enjoyed his battles, he always looked for more.
"Manu ad ferrum" – his nickname told it all,
His ferocity held everyone in thrall.
He was determined Rome should be restored,
Her authority throughout the Empire by none ignored.
Italy he set to peace and then in Illyria
He overcame the Goths and now to Syria

DIOCLETIAN

He comes in glory and elemental power
That all bow down, abase themselves and cower
And Queen Zenobia with the greatest and the least
Shall accept the imperial writ throughout the East.
The war went well till Tyana refused to yield,
Before the Cilician Gates it held a shield;
The citizens of Tyana had sworn to block
This way across the Taurus to Antioch.

And now was the time the detachment from the Tenth arrived
As against Tyana Aurelian's legions strived.
The detachment commander reported, his place assigned,
The siege engines ready and all the walls were mined.

The Emperor declared Tyana now must fall.
His furious threats were heard by one and all,
"There won't be left even a dog alive!"
The terrified citizens doubted if they'd survive;
The soldiers dreamt of booty as they prepared
For the massive assault so no one would be spared.

But the soldiers were thwarted – it happened in this way:
There was a traitor who'd promised to betray
The people of Tyana, goods and wealth –
He'd show a way which could be seized by stealth –
But just as all expected a worthwhile fight
The Emperor had the strangest dream that night:
He saw Apollonius the philosopher standing by his bed
And he heard his voice afar from the land of the dead:

"Aurelian –
If you wish to conquer you do not have to kill
For remove men's fear then loyalty you'll instil.
Aurelian –
If you wish to rule all innocent blood avoid,
Who rule by blood, are by blood destroyed.
Aurelian –
If you wish to live for long in the world of the living
Act with mercy to all, and for ever be forgiving."

Aurelian rose early and pondered long his dream,
For in spite of his nature he was impressed by its theme.
Three times the philosopher had made his message clear:
In ruling, kindness has more effect than fear.

AURELIAN THE EXAMPLE

The traitor came to guide him through the maze,
Through defensive earthworks till on the town they gaze.
They were on a rock standing above Tyana
And there Aurelian planted the imperial banner.
The amazéd citizens saw him standing there
Seeming alone in the city, without a fear –
A magnificent sight standing in the morning sun
All gleaming in his armour – then slowly one by one
The citizens came to greet him as their lord
To swear allegiance of their own accord.

The army saw him standing there alone,
Came charging through the way the traitor'd shown.
Now was the time for booty, pillage and rape
The soldiers searched the town that none escape.
But the Emperor recalled his vision and its demand;
He called his men to order with this command:
"No looting, for Tyana has my word,
The city has sworn allegiance to me, their lord."
The soldiers grumbled, thwarted of their prey,
But the fickleness of crowds was seen that day,
For the Emperor laughed and exclaimed unto his men:
"My word's my bond. No dog shall live! So then
Go find the dogs and string them up straightway!"
And laughingly the Emperor's men obey.
Tyana's saved; and the army forced the pass
And entered the plain with its streams and verdant grass.

And what of the traitor, I hear you enquire,
What gifts and presents did that man acquire,
Who'd saved the Emperor from a costly fight?
He dreamt of honours, riches, his by right,
But Aurelian reverting to his normal self
Declared he hated traitors and their stealth –
"Remove him from my presence without delay.
In fact remove his head – At once, I say!"

This was the tale of Aurelian which Diocles heard
Which made him realise the power of an Emperor's word;
He thought – He spoke – and Fate was thus fulfilled,
For the people of Tyana were saved and the dogs killed.

DIOCLETIAN

The Battle for Antioch   AD 272
aet. 28

The Army of Aurelian forced the Syrian Gates.
See now the opposition that awaits,
Impeding his progress, holding his power at bay,
So Zenobia's general Zabdas will delay
His approach to Antioch. The road is barred
By armoured horse and by the royal guard,
All massed on the River Orontes further bank
With archers and mercenaries set on either flank.

The Emperor Aurelian who'd once been Master of Horse
Well understood how cavalry can be the source
Of an army's power flexible in defence and attack;
Was very aware of the Palmyrene's famed cataphract,
The effect as armoured men and horses charge,
They pierce the line, small breakthroughs they enlarge.
He needs must blunt this weapon to succeed
In defeating Zabdas that Antioch may be freed.

Aurelian with his staff survey the scene
Southward the city, the Orontes in between.
"We must protect the infantry from the cataphracts
                                      and limit their loss
We must establish a bridgehead and get the cavalry across,
For the victory – we can safely rely on them to deliver,
And we'll keep the infantry on this side of the river."

At once there were murmurs and doubts among the staff
For according to military lore, an army's but half
As effective a force when divided and split in two parts.
The Emperor then proved how brilliance so often departs
From the mundane attempts of everyday ordinary men
In the way that problems get solved again and again.

"Summon the commanders of all the legionary horse.
The Mauritanian Lancers are required as well of course.
Is their Prefect here? Now pay attention please.
Carefully follow this plan. The prize we will seize,
By using their strength and the heat of the midday sun;
Antioch will be ours before the day is done."

The officers listened and thought, then shouted with glee,
"We'll follow this plan, and the Palmyrene army must flee!"

AURELIAN THE EXAMPLE

— ✵ —

The early sun just touched the city towers
As Zabdas surveyed the Roman army's powers
There to the East, massed cavalry rank on rank,
But the legions lined the river's northern bank.
The cataphracts then, troop by troop appear,
Full armoured, sharp of axe and pennoned spear.
A terrifying sight for all to contemplate,
The unending stream comes through the city gate.
Slowly they form their formidable array;
The men and horses and massive armour weigh
So much the tremendous force of their charge impacts
All those who stand against the cataphracts.

Slowly they form; the sun climbs in the sky,
The enemy seems to dance before the eye
As haze and dust obscure the morning view;
The Romans wonder what may now ensue.

The Palmyrene army parades in full array,
The might of Zenobia, a magnificent display.
The cataphracts present an armoured wall
Which makes veterans to pause, recruits appal.
The Palmyrene infantry posted on the river flank
Watch the legions on the Orontes' northern bank.
A trumpet sounds and then a pennant's dropped,
The armoured line with gleaming helms attopped
Get under way, keeping their line in place,
Approach more quickly, now they seem to race,
Thundering down the plain, an awful sight;
How can the Roman horse resist their might?

As the Palmyrene wave seems just about to crash
On the lighter Roman horse, and them to smash,
The Romans withdraw but not in disarray
Maintaining formation and thus the plan obey.
Each time the heavy armoured horse approached
The Roman cavalry withdrew as they'd been coached;
They kept their line tempting the cataphracts
To charge again, repeating their attacks.

DIOCLETIAN

The day was now half done, the heat intense,
The Palmyrenes with their armour weight immense
Began to falter, then to slowly tire.
Where now are those mighty warriors who awe inspire?
Drooping they stood, horses and men at bay,
Completely unable to charge again that day.

Another trumpet sounds on the Roman side,
The Roman horse prepare to turn the tide
The exhausted cataphracts can only stand
Bemused they look and hardly lift a hand.

And then there was a fearsome killing done
Of Palmyrenes weary in the heat of the midday sun.
The Army of Queen Zenobia melted away
Before Aurelian on that triumphant day.

The Battle for Emesa

Aurelian pressing southward along the Orontes
Is welcomed at every city which he frees.
Before Emesa, where the Sun God dwells,
Whose awful power throughout the world compels
The worship of everyone from every land,
Here the Queen and Zabdas turn and stand.
A mighty army, seventy thousand strong
Outnumber Aurelian in spite of all his throng
Of mercenary troops and diverse federates
Supplied along the way by towns and states.

No river here protects the Roman foot,
Therefore the cavalry on either flank are put.
The battle opens with a thunderous charge,
The armoured cataphracts and horses large
The lighter Roman horse cannot withdraw,
And exhaust the cataphracts as they did before,
For fear that the Palmyrene forces will surround
And engulf the Romans and so win the ground.

Above the noise and chaos shines the Sun;
The fiery eye sees all and everyone,

AURELIAN THE EXAMPLE

How some fight well and others quake with fear,
The sweep of sword, the cries, the lunge of spear,
The sweat, the stink, the grunts, the gasps for breath,
The shouts of triumph and the cries of death.

The Roman horse seemed just about to break,
Just one more charge the Palmyrenes had to make.
The legions struggled grimly hand to hand,
Borne down by heat, they almost were unmanned,
Then a federate armed with club and stave
Struck out by chance and did the army save.
Which of the gods inspired the man, who knows?
Which god did they invoke as battering blows,
His fellows followed him, the charge was stopped.
The Palestinian clubmen smashed and chopped
The Palmyrene armoured horse into the ground,
Nowhere to turn, no haven to be found.
All exhausted, under the setting sun,
Victors and vanquished all stood there undone;
And through the haze the Roman soldiers saw
Angels of some god helping their war.
Surely power divine was used that day
To help the Romans triumph in the fray.

Rest after Battle

AD 272
aet. 28

It is dark, but the warmth of the day lingers on;
It is night, overhead all the stars sharply shine.
All around there's the light of army camp fires;
By one there's a group of centurions collected
Discussing the affairs of their elders and betters,
With opinion and knowledge based soundly on gossip,
Which flourishes healthily in armies at rest.

"What a man! What a general, our Aurelian is.
It was alone due to him, that Tyana fell.
Did you see him there in the morning sun?
Like a god. Standing tall. For all to see."

Diocles was listening, sitting out of the light;
He asked the enthusiast, in his quiet voice –

DIOCLETIAN

A voice which demanded at all times attention,
Attention to one who thought long and thought deep:
"But tell me, what if on that glorious morn
A Tyana archer had seen the Emperor,
And promptly with a well aimed bolt had fixed
Aurelian, the Orient, and the Empire – all.

It is passing hard to be an Emperor
And perform the duties of a general too.
In one you have to think of many things
And see how everything affects the other,
Meanwhile the general has a single aim,
Dangerous indeed, but simple overall."

"That I can't accept. You saw the man –
How he seized the chance without delay
When the Palestinian federate turned
And clubbed by merest chance the cataphract.
Half blind with sweat our man in frenzy struck
Everything around him and by chance
Completely felled the armoured man and horse.

Aurelian in the very thick of things,
He understood exactly what he saw –
He saw the way to stop the cataphracts;
He called on the men to turn and face their flank,
To batter the Palmyrene to utter pulp."

"But that's my point, exactly what I mean.
That is the act of greatest generalship.
He seized the chance, the briefest fleeting chance,
Made clear by long and hard experience.
However the aim has always been the same,
To defeat the foe, and so impose ones will.
Hard and dangerous work without a doubt
But simple too because there's but one aim.

To me it's foolish to put the world at risk
In every battle, skirmish and foray.
One needs I think, to keep the two apart,
The Emperor and the General must be split;
Yet each their authority and power derives
From us, the Roman army, that's for sure,

AURELIAN THE EXAMPLE

So how can we have an emperor overall,
With a general there to fight his wars for him,
Who is not also tempted to fight his master?"

A voice broke in: "Diocles, enough!
You theorise too much for most of us."

The voice went on to tell the latest news.
"The Emperor's gone, I hear, to sacrifice
In Emesa, at the Temple of the Sun."

"As indeed he should," another said,
"I have no doubt at all the victorious Sun
Was very active on our side that day.
Lucius of the fourth saw them himself…"

"Saw what?" another asked, "What did he see?"

"He saw the angels fighting in the line.
Brighter than burnished brass is what he said,
And where they went, so we followed through."

Diocles considered carefully how they felt:
The need of all for some superior power,
The final fount of all authority,
Served by Emperor, peasant, everyone.
This was indeed the ultimate paradox –
Greater the power the Emperor seeks to wield,
The greater his need to serve a greater power.
Indeed an Emperor's not an easy task.

One by one the comrades said goodnight;
Some to their tents, others by starlight slept;
All was quiet, only the slightest breeze,
And the muffled sounds of many men asleep.

ZENOBIA
in which Diocles finds himself close to imperial power

Zenobia wept –
And in fury brushed away her tears.
She'd not be cowed –
And frustrated, laughed in anger at the thought.
Never had been cowed
Not even by Odanathus in his prime.
Here fast confined
Within Palmyra's walls, all that remained
Of grandest dreams
Of dominating half the known world.
But why? Oh why?
She'd overcome her woman's frailty,
And done much more;
She'd triumphed in the busy world of men,
And equalled them;
Now as an equal found herself confined –
Zenobia alone.

The Queen's Council

PALMYRA
AD 272
aet. 28

The taper flickered on the ill-lit wall,
The audience chamber all in disarray,
When General Zabdas to the council came,
The last to join the advisers of the Queen,

DIOCLETIAN

Here summoned, at short notice, from the walls,
Where he had been directing the defence
Of Queen Zenobia's final hiding place,
Palmyra, city set in the desert sands.
In spite of all the chaos everywhere
Still Zenobia royally dominates
All those around her, waiting on her voice.
There on the dais which makes her doubly tall,
The one bright torch illuminates her form,
Her noble head, imperious eyes, her stance,
Impress on all the epitome of power,
Which once seen, none ever can forget.

In contrast to the Queen, her council stand,
As men in midst of business incomplete,
Caught unawares by summons to the court,
Some still with dirt and stench of battle reek,
While others carry records, tallies, pens,
For the bureaucracy must be maintained,
Even when the Palmyrene empire's on the brink
Of final extinction at Aurelian's hand.

The General Zabdas approaches, bows and waits,
The Queen nods slightly, then the Chamberlain
In tones made stately by long use at court,
Calls the council to order and the meeting starts.

"Know you Her Majesty the Queen's received
A message from the Augustus Aurelian.
Her Majesty requires your loyal advice
How best to answer for our general good."

An excited murmur among the counsellors:
"What letter's this? What does it say? When came?"
The rush and interruptions of the siege
Have breached the informal information lines
Essential to effective government.
Hush. The Queen speaks and with respect
Her courtiers wait on every phrase and tone
To guess what's in her mind, for how they'll speak
Is influenced as much by what they fear
As what they think – these courtiers loyal and wise.

ZENOBIA

"Know then my friends and colleagues... [Courtier beware!
When seeming equal, she is most dangerous.]
That I've received a missive from my brother...
[She calls him 'brother' who's her enemy;
By this she claims equality with Rome.
Beware. At court it's deadly dangerous.]
I need your help how best to answer this
So we can turn the tide and reign again."

Following the custom as in many courts,
The junior first must speak, then rank on rank
Progressively the more experienced give
Their advice to the Queen so she at length collects
A consensus of the opinions of her lords,
Then gives her ruling, while each counsellor
Recalls how close his words were to the Queen's –
Distinct but close, the art of counselling.

But all are at a loss for none have seen
The contents of the letter just received.
As the junior hesitates about to plunge
Into the mire of guess and prejudice,
The noble Cassius Longinus intervenes,
As on occasion he has done before,
Bringing sweet reasonableness and common sense
Into the hysteric climate of the court.

"Madam, I am sure you desire sound counsel now
At this stage of crisis in Palmyra's growth,
For grow it will if the right choice is made
And sound advice is midwife to right choice.
If the Lord Chamberlain might read to us the letter,
Then each and everyone of us can think
How best you should respond to gain such time
Needed to restore the fortunes of your house."

The Queen nods slightly and the Chamberlain,
Officiously adjusting his gown, proceeds to read:
"Aurelianus Imperator Romani Orbis etcetera
Recoverer of all the East to Zenobia, Greetings,
Also to federates and Zenobia's other allies
[He gives the Queen no title at all, you note]

DIOCLETIAN

You should have done by now of your free will
All that which in this letter I do command.
Immediately your surrender I require.
I promise, one and all, I will spare your lives
Provided that Zenobia and her sons
Shall dwell wherever the Senate stipulates
Which I will designate as they may wish.
Your gold, your silver, horses, camels, wealth
Shall to the treasury be at once transferred.
May the people of Palmyra rest assured
Their rights shall be preserved as heretofore.
[And those desiring peace, heard this for sure.]
Given this day at Emesa by my hand
Aurelianus Augustus Imperator etcetera etcetera."

The murmuring grew apace with each new point,
Desperately the Chamberlain "Order! Order!" cried
Reminding counsellors they are in duty bound
To help the Queen compose a fair reply
So entered then the councils' ritual round
Beginning with the humblest present there
Progressing to the seniors, one by one.

Some spoke of peace and need to compromise,
Others leaned to action fierce and proud
Ignoring Palmyra's present parlous state.
The politicians noticed that the Queen
Smiled more on these than on the careful ones,
So gradually the general mood there in the room
Inclined to brave rejection of the note,
Until Longinus took his turn to speak.

"Great noble Queen, I've served you loyal and long
Since the day I came from Athens to your court,
From academic life in theory fixed,
To the practical and raw exigencies of court,
Tutor at first and then your counsellor,
Freedom I loved and taught you freedom too.
Your break with Rome I backed. You could be free
Of Rome and Persia both. Zenobia alone.

ZENOBIA

But we did not reckon on Aurelian,
That animal power exploding from the west.
All our proudest troops he has laid low,
They say the very gods give him support.
The time has come, I think, to compromise.
Dead men cannot be free, not in this world;
Soft answers will give time, time to be free,
Time to ride to Ctesiphon for help."

The Queen half heard the noble man's advice
And half her mind dwelt on those golden days,
The days when she with Odenathus ruled
The eastern world as delegates of Rome,
But at such remove effectively were free,
Free to live and free. But wanted more
And Odenathus died, alone she ruled
And broke with Rome… what's that Longinus said?

And as often happens with the best advice
Only half is heard and that half understood.
Meanwhile the council's business must be done
Immediate work to do. The Queen decides.

"A missive such as this I have never had
And never will. The answer I will draft.
Good Cassius Longinus have it well prepared,
Translate the letter into Grecian form
That Aurelian may know how to address a Queen.
Meanwhile the fastest dromedaries prepare.
Early tomorrow I will ride to Persia,
And with their help, Palmyra's great again."

Zenobia's Letter

AD 272
aet. 28

"From Zenobia, Queen of the East, to Aurelian Augustus.
None have demanded by letter what now you are demanding.
Whatever in war is achieved, it must be by valour.
In your ignorance now you demand my surrender not knowing
You are addressing the last of the line of Queen Cleopatra,
Who preferred as a monarch to die than to humbly continue.
We lack not for friends or for federates, their help is at hand,
The brigands of Syria attack you, your army is starving.

DIOCLETIAN

Shortly your troubles will mount and your pride be deflated;
You will never again try a letter instead of your valour."

Trembling, the Emperor's secretary read again,
He sought the slightest hint of compromise.
He knew his master wished to end this war,
Momentum lost before Palmyra's walls.
The Emperor's letter, fierce as it might sound,
Had been intended as the opening ploy
In a negotiated settlement of peace.
The secretary cunningly drafted it as such
And in spite of all his plans – the answer this!

But it came to pass that when Aurelian
Had Queen Zenobia's proud reply read loud,
In front of all the court and military men,
He felt relief and laughed for all to hear.
Gone were the inhibitions that he had felt
When fate decreed he must a woman fight.
Immediately the Emperor Aurelian called his staff
And planned how best to intensify the seige;
Sent some to parley with the brigand chiefs
And gain support by buying their supplies;
And others sent to cut the Persian line
To prevent more help coming from the East.

Meanwhile the secretary, a careful politic man,
Congratulates himself, who had prepared this scheme,
He, who had drafted such a careful letter,
Which had produced such a satisfactory end.

The Capture of the Queen

AD 272
aet. 28

You know that time just before the dawn
When objects take on shape in shades of grey,
And gradually colour seeps back into things,
Familiar objects for another day.

Such was the time with Palmyra half asleep,
Surrounded by the Roman picket line,
A shadow indistinct is all that shows,
As someone tries to break the close confine.

ZENOBIA

The day relief had occupied the post,
Diocles' men had already left for camp,
When there he saw in the half light fleetingly
A movement from the postern by the ramp.

Already it had gone, lost in the gloom,
No time to doubt or question what to do,
He turned his horse, called to his optio:
"You take command. This shadow I'll pursue".

Passing his comrade from the next in line,
"Come with me," he called, "we have work to do."
Diocles and Maximian rode to the dawn
Trying to keep the shadowy forms in view.

As sun came up investing all with life
And gradual warmth on all that could be seen,
They saw a troop of speeding dromedaries flee,
An escort with the standard of the Queen.

The Great Aurelian roared with furious rage
When told that Queen Zenobia had fled the town.
"Stand to, the Mauritanian Lancers, ride,
Go ride with all despatch, go ride her down."

The two centurions showing them the way,
The Lancers pell-mell down the road, career.
Exhausted, on the second day they reach
The Euphrates river, but there is no-one there.

A felucca, almost stationary, midstream,
By wind and tide in uneasy balance held,
Making the ship a virtual prisoner,
And there on board Zenobia they beheld.

Diocles could see further up the bank
Two lighter skiffs which hastily they board,
Using the stream to bring them quickly down
They storm the larger boat with fire and sword.

Triumphant to Palmyra they return,
There Queen Zenobia in their midst is seen.
The Emperor Aurelian condescends to grant
A resting place for this so restless Queen.

DIOCLETIAN

Later an officer of the Imperial Staff
Told the two centurions to report
To the Emperor straightaway for he has asked to see
The men who brought Zenobia to court.

And so our heroes approached the Emperor,
Congratulated on their speed of thought
Which had frustrated the restless Queen's designs
And brought her cunning strategies to nought.

And for their part in this action they were made
Both members of the elite Protector corps.
They "adored the purple" on that auspicious day
And served the Emperor loyally evermore.

The Trial of Zenobia

EMESA
AD 272
aet. 28

From where I stand, I can see it all:
The banners of the legions decked in gold,
The dragon-flags of federates all aglow,
Each held aloft by officers in their place
Appointed by the Master of the Court.
They form a wall of jewelled and glorious signs,
A backdrop for the Emperor's throne on high
Above the court where all the supplicants wait;
And on each side we stand in dress parade,
The Protectors of the Emperor, rank on rank,
Our helmets, breastplates, all, are burnished bright,
Together with the standards set the scene,
Await the revelation yet to come
Of the Emperor Aurelian, saviour of the world.

A trumpet sounds – the Protectors stand to attention.
From the corner of my eye, I can just see
The imperial entourage busily approach.
The lictors first in single file proceed,
Their rods of office all with laurel decked,
Then follow those who backwards walk, and show
With sweep of arm and bended knee, the way
To the great Augustus, glorious to see,
With radiate crown and purple cloak, whose sheen

ZENOBIA

Is such that all about do fade to ash,
A Persian gift, of Indian sandyx made,
Of purple hue which none again shall find,
Aurelian, the very embodiment of god.

The mighty Emperor, with his radiate crown,
The Sun God does resemble more and more,
Emesa's god, which in the battle strove
In our support that we might overcome.
Now, I, Diocles understand why all
This ceremony's essential, to support
The ultimate authority of the Emperor
And reinforce his sacred difference.

My mind has wandered, but my body's still
At strict attention, standing near the throne,
As now the Emperor approaches, turns, and sits,
And all the court responds by bowing low.
Again the trumpets sound, and from afar
There sounds again a further trumpet call,
Then gradually through the great door of the hall
Appears the party of Palmyra's Queen,
We now will witness the last and final act
In Zenobia's struggle against the power of Rome.

With solemn pomp the Palmyrenes take their place,
And then the Master of the Court stands forth:
"Know that the Emperor Aurelian has decreed
That Queen Zenobia must herself stand trial
For claiming independence for her son,
And flouting Rome's authority in the East."
(In fact he spoke much longer to this end;
Standing stiffly here the blood drains from my head –
Rocking forward off my heels will ease the flow –
I must remember all I see and hear.)

Then the prosecution advocate presents
With many a word and high flown legal phrase
The Imperial case against the Palmyrenes,
How the Queen has ignored the former agreements and rights
Under which her husband had held the East for Rome,
Had taken Egypt and cut off the supplies of corn

DIOCLETIAN

So critical for the crowded cities of the West –
"The sentence for usurping power is clear –
We ask the judgement of the court — her death."

Then noble Cassius Longinus takes the stand
And speaks in defence of Queen Zenobia
"I humbly would remind you, great Aurelian,
At the time the ill-fated Emperor Valerian fell
Into the hands of Sapor, king of kings,
(His fall reminds us all until this day
How fragile is the fortune of us all.
One day on high with all accoutrements
Of power and wealth, and then adversity
Reduces each of us unto ourselves;
Then you know exactly what you are worth.)

[The Emperor flushed with anger, he scowled at the man.
Why remind the Emperor of the chance of things?]

That same Sapor he then attacked this town,
And but for Odenathus would have set
The Persian frontier here in Syria.
Brave Odenathus forced Sapor to flee.
He seized his treasure and his royal wives,
He re-established the authority of Rome,
Which fact your predecessors recognised
By granting him the titles and the rank
Of Imperator and Dux Romanorum.
Undoubtedly this same Odenathus saved
The Roman power here in the Orient;
And when he died authority was transferred
To Queen Zenobia, guardian to their son.
What powers she held, she held in trust for Rome,
And if it seems she has made excessive claims,
It was of necessity to keep the peace
For Rome and also for Palmyra too,
Because by former treaties all our aims
And interests are one, to hold the East
Against the armies of the Persian king.
I humbly submit therefore, my noble Lord,
The Queen deserves not death but recompense
For all her efforts spent to hold the East."

ZENOBIA

The Emperor's anger grew with every word.
Longinus offered no defence at all,
But rather did his argument aggravate
The parlous situation of the Queen.
From where I stood, his fury evident,
I saw him turn to his secretary Mucapor,
On whom he lent for comment and advice
On matters civil and political;
And then the Master of the Court was called;
A few more words and then the Master turned,
Declared the court recessed until next day.

Much of the rest I gleaned from talk at court,
And from my observations here and there.
Mucapor called upon the Queen that night,
Explained that she was in a desperate strait,
And Longinus' plea had just made matters worse,
But that the Emperor desired not for her death,
He would rather that she quietly should retire,
If a scapegoat could be found to save his face.
Mucapor thus far strictly had fulfilled
His master's orders, but now he added this,
An extra twist as servants often do,
To satisfy that jealousy and hate
For which he had held Longinus many years.
He gave the distraught Queen to understand
Longinus was the price that must be paid.

And so it was upon the following day,
We were paraded as we were before.
I still recall the murmur in the crowd,
The moment the Queen Zenobia alone stood forth,
For this broke custom, ceremony, ritual, all.
The Queen would speak herself without the aid
Of advocate or other form of help.
And what she said surprised us even more,
(For no one knew what Mucapor had arranged),
She claimed to have been led astray by those
Who wished to see her son increase his power
All at the expense of Ctesiphon and Rome,
And this she had not prevented because of love,
A Mother's love which led her further astray.

DIOCLETIAN

"Who counselled thus? Who had led the Queen astray?
And what of that bold letter which she had sent?
How came this to be written in such a vein?"
"The Queen did merely draft it in her tongue,
And others wrote the final form in Greek."
"And who did that?" And so it was, at length,
That noble Cassius Longinus appeared to all
To be the one, who had led the Queen astray;
And this he did not deny, perhaps rejoiced
To be the Queen's scapegoat, that she be free,
Calmly accepting the imperial sentence of death.

But still I wonder why it came to pass
Exactly as it did, and what it taught
About the essential rules of politics.
To be effective and survive to rule
An Emperor must be seen to be aloof;
How knows he then all that comes to pass?
It is easy for a few to form a group
Around his throne, and keep him in the dark.
Thus Mucapor sought his own private designs
Rather than following his master's strict desires.

Why did that noble woman do what she did?
Disloyalty breeds disloyalty, that is for sure.
The scapegoat is to me a mystery.
Even now, I know there is much more to learn
From those first days with great Aurelian.

PREPARATION
**in which Diocles recognises his ambition
and plans to prepare himself for imperial power**

The Fated Boar

TUNGRIA
AD 274
aet. 30

It was a dull day, they had not seen the sun,
Half-hearted rain, cold for the time of year;
With summer gone, the days were shortening fast;
They looked for shelter in the growing gloom.

That was the year the great Aurelian
Had re-established imperial power in Gaul
So Rome's authority stretched throughout the world.
"Restitur Orbis" he had been proclaimed,
Had now returned in glorious triumph to Rome
With all the rebel rulers in his train.
Aurelian "sword in hand" had saved the state.

It still continued dull and cold in Gaul
And the evening light was disappearing fast,
Aurelian's officers knew they needed warmth
And anxiously rode into the deepening night.

Gaul had been for many years apart,
With local generals usurping authority.
With their attention half the time on Rome,
The northern frontier had not been firmly held.

The German nations recognised their chance
And many times broke through the frontier line
And invaded Gaul sacking the open towns,

DIOCLETIAN

Returning with plunder safe across the Rhine.
To give the northern frontier greater strength,
It was withdrawn south of the River Waal
And now stood east and west in Tungrian land
Leaving an open zone towards the north.
So when the Lord Aurelian regained control
He sent staff officers to the north to check
That all was well within the defensive zone,
And that the tribes realised Aurelian ruled.

The Emperor in his majesty decides,
His chief-of-staff and lesser generals choose
The officers who in detail implement –
And so these two sought shelter in the night.

"Is that a light, Maximian, that I see?
Or is it yet another will o' the wisp?
On nights like this whole armies have been lost
Drowned without a trace in the Batavian swamp."

"Courage Diocles! We'll do more than drown
Obscurely in a swamp in northern Gaul.
What have we here? – An inn! All fully stocked,
Stabling for horses, food and bed for us."

They knock and enter the simple smoke-filled room –
"You see two travellers in need of bed and board
And stabling for their horses and provender."

"That I can do – I'll call the boy at once
To take the horses and I'll prepare a meal."

Then the other spoke, "Maximian, hold hard.
First let us know the tariff of this inn.
I hate to commit myself in ignorance
And have to argue when the account is made."

But Maximian laughed; he was already by the fire,
Caring not the cost, relaxing in the warmth.
Diocles smiled – he did not push the point –
He joined his friend and waited for his meal.

And so they stayed there at the lonely inn
The eight days they needed to complete their task,
To see without being seen how well the guards

PREPARATION

Fulfilled their duties on the Tungrian line,
And then most carefully with the Franks conferred
To ensure they fully understood the change
Which great Aurelian's regaining power entailed.

While they did this, the widow at the inn
Watched them with increased interest and concern.
Her gift of second sight had been a trial
Since as a child, she had with druids dwelt.
She would see the death of someone precisely clear
With all the horror and the pain to come,
Or see a knife used by a man to eat
Which tomorrow will kill a neighbour in a brawl.

She observed how Diocles carefully watched and planned;
How Maximian would rush in and afterwards turn
And ask his partner then what he should do!
How Diocles assessed the border garrison,
Recording with care their sharpness and their skill,
And with the Franks his great authority
As he impressed on them the power of Rome.
But she noticed too how his friend's impetuousness,
Helped Diocles to perform his work.
For Diocles often preferred to come behind
So he might see the effects and then could plan
How best to achieve the ultimate success.

The eight days passed and gradually they became
More familiar with each other, friendly too.
There was great laughter in the yard one day
When the fattening pig broke loose and chased them all,
The boys and workmen – everyone jumped clear,
None faster than Diocles passing by.
"Thank god, it wasn't a boar," the pigman cried.

The widow at the doorstep saw it all,
Trained as she was to know the ancient signs –
The boar significant in her peoples' past –
And then she saw... an Army, rank on rank,
Paraded there before a tribunal.
Her lodger Diocles stands for all to see,
Another in chains – a question asked – a shout –

DIOCLETIAN

The briefest flash of fear in Diocles' eye,
And then he draws his sword, holds it on high...
All fades... it is the yard in Tungria,
And the continued squealing of the furious pig.

On parting next day when they called for their reckoning
Diocles questioned every detailed charge;
That this was his very nature she had observed.
"You're far too stingy Diocles for an officer!"
He showed his purse and laughingly shook his head,
"When I am emperor I'll be more generous."

And then she saw the army, rank on rank,
And Diocles there alone, his sword in hand.
"Diocles do not jest, for you will become
The Emperor when you have slain your fated boar!"

There was a pause – Diocles held his peace,
Straightway he knew that this was his desire.
He could succeed, must prepare for what's in store,
But first must seek and kill the fated boar.

Thoughts, Rank on Rank

EGYPT
AD 275
aet. 31

"I was in Alexandria when I heard the news,
The news that the great Aurelian was dead,
I recall my feelings, as if it were yesterday,
For he was the very first Emperor that I had known.
It was he that made me a protector, him I served,
And from him I learnt much of that special art
Of leading men and being an Emperor
By what he did, and by what he failed to do –
For he was flawed but nonetheless was great,
Great in making men fear Rome again.
"Restitur Orbis" rightly he was called,
But his wrath was something terrible to see.
All men feared him, and fear it was in the end
Which was the cause of great Aurelian's death.

The news brought in its wake a trail of thoughts.
It was as if they had been waiting there,
Waiting for this single fact to set them free

PREPARATION

To join together and bring certainty –
Just as disparate units on the march
Brought together make a striking force,
An army with one leader and one aim
To seek and utterly to destroy the foe,
So in my mind these thoughts formed rank on rank
Till I was certain what I had to do.

First, here I was in Alexandria,
The City named for the greatest king of all.
And by my age, he had finished his life's work –
But by my age, he had been undone,
Dead of a fever in far off Babylon,
But by that age what had I achieved?
A protector on the staff of General Probus
Sent to Alexandria for stores,
While the General campaigned further to the south –
But I also remember feeling that I lived
And Alexander was dead – I still had time.

And then another thought, there are no boars
Here on the coast or by the river Nile.
I cannot forget that Inn in Tungria –
The strange regard of the widow's distant eye.
She'd made me certain why I am alive,
And everything I must do to achieve my goal –
But straightway I am sent with Probus here
To the land of Egypt, a place bereft of boars!

Then of Aurelian, very much alive,
A man whose animal force made others pale.
His energy was a part of Nature's store
As basic as the tempest or the flood
And just as dangerous for all those who stood
Between the fierce Aurelian and his desires.
And those desires were largely justified,
That Rome should be respected once again,
That commerce flourish and the land be tilled,
That all acknowledge the overarching Sun.
This same God who at Emesa fought
And helped him overcome Zenobia,
He worshipped in the very heart of Rome –

DIOCLETIAN

And yet he failed. His energy uncontrolled
Exploded in his wrath whenever crossed
Or however briefly he was held in check
And this untrammelled wrath did him undo.

They say his frightened secretary planned the plot;
He who had worked for Aurelian many years
Was found in some default and feared the worst,
So he forged lists of names to make the staff
Believe Aurelian meant to punish them.
Fearing for their lives these men conspired together
And murdered him as the Army marched through Thrace.

And then my thoughts formed in their ordered ranks,
I still have time, but needs must plan that time
If I am to achieve what Alexander did.
But it is a different ruler which we need,
Someone with the energy of Aurelian,
But with control, and wisdom to choose men
Who will perform the necessary tasks
To ensure the Empire survives a thousand years.

I am that man, but cannot reach the throne
Unless I prepare myself and learn the skills –
I need command of men on the frontier line,
Because to gain the purple 'one' requires –
The ambitious thought is too fearful to say 'I' –
Requires the common soldiers' approbation
And the approval of all the army's senior ranks.
Therefore to be widely known I must have command
Far enough from the Emperor to be free,
But close enough to have my actions seen,
And if it proves to be good hunting land,
So much the better if there are boars to hand."

Lament

No more the sword in hand,
No more the battle charge,
No more the call to war,
Aurelian is dead.

PREPARATION

Who now will rule the land,
Who now our lives enlarge
And raise our spirits more?
Aurelian is dead.

The Barbarians rejoice,
No longer need they fear
The authority of Rome.
Aurelian is dead.

No more we'll hear his voice,
Above the war sound clear
Driving the onslaught home.
Aurelain is dead.

Silence after storm,
Desolation after flood,
Darkness after fire.
Aurelian is dead.

Who will the world transform,
Who will find new blood,
Who will men inspire?
Aurelian is dead.

No more the sword in hand,
No more the battle charge,
Aurelian is no more.
Aurelian is dead.

Conversation Piece

Egypt
AD 276
aet. 32

"I needs must get a wife…"

"But why, Diocles, why?"

"Life is full and opportunities abound,
Each problem, interlocking with the next
Is there to solve, and each solution sweet,
But sweeter yet to have a son to share…"

"And if a daughter, then?"

"I'd love her too,
And she would bear fine sons to follow on…"

DIOCLETIAN

"But there be risks…"

                "Maximian, I forgot!
Wrapped in my dreams – your loss – your daughter's safe
In the household of your dear wife's family? –
But I think it's time I found myself a wife."

"And Diocles, knowing you, you probably will.
Marriage I think is more than heritance.
I knew more joy and assurance in those months
Than in all the years…"

                "That, I can believe,
But I have need to experience it for myself."

Sirmium in the Fall   AD 276
aet. 32

It was late in the summer in Sirmium,
When the Army of the Oriént
Arrived with the Emperor Probus,
On rest and pleasure bent.

Excitement in those households
With daughters yet to wed,
Mothers, aunts, observed the field
And many palms were read.

"Will you marry young my dear?
How many for a start?
Do you seek a younger man,
Or one who is young at heart?"

So the good ladies of Sirmium
Made ready to enjoy
The brief surplus of single men,
Their cunning wiles employ.

So it was in Priscus' house,
His ladies were a flutter.
Dealt with his natural diffidence,
Like a knife through butter.

PREPARATION

Priscus had been a centurion once,
And reached the highest rank.
He knew his worth, and those about,
Took care with whom he drank.

But encouraged by his womenfolk,
He chanced his arm for once.
He asked the Imperial staff to dine,
Risking their affronts.

Some junior members of the staff,
To dine did condescend,
And there was our Diocles,
With Maximian, his friend.

And so young Prisca found her man
At Sirmium in the fall,
Little knowing, she would become
Wife of the Lord of All.

Certainty AD 276
aet. 32

I saw him standing there. I knew.
He was for me, and had been so
Since time had been a little child.
My name deep etched upon his heart,
And his on mine.

And watching thus, the link it grew
As strong as any chain you know.
He looked so fierce until he smiled.
And so of me, he took a part,
And us entwine.

And why that one and not the rest?
In an instant you realise
With that certainty the gods allow
Once in your life if you seize the chance,
You know your fate.

DIOCLETIAN

A man enthralled upon a quest
Seeking to learn, already wise,
A man who has need of me – and now.
I knew for sure, just by his glance.
I cannot wait.

An Old Man Remembers

AD 276
aet. 32

"I knew the Emperor once. I knew him well.
Plain Diocles then – was long ago.
And here we are in the far flung Caucasus
Watching and waiting for the next barbarian raid.
My god, it's cold – so different from that night
At Sirmium in the fall, when we were young.

You don't believe me – that I knew him well?
That was the year that Probus came to power.
There had been the usual struggle to succeed;
He had won, and then marched west and fought the Goths,
And after that he came to Sirmium –
October was unseasonably warm that year.
The womenfolk, whatever their degree,
Became concerned with wardrobes, fashions, paint,
The news at court, what Probus liked to eat;
And we of the garrison, at first we laughed,
But then the inevitable jealousy reared its head –
With brawls in taverns, troubles at the races.
This got so bad that a conference was called…
And where does the great Diocletian come in, you ask?
Patience my friend. The night is young. There's time.

Now where was I? The conference – yes. I went
With other officers from the garrison,
And there among the imperial staff, was one
Whose authority came not from his official rank,
But rather from few words and questions asked,
And the way his senior colleagues consulted him,
And regularly listened. We commented on this.
I forget the details of what was then agreed,
But suffice to say, afterwards all was calm
Between the various units in the town.

PREPARATION

Now I knew a veteran there in Sirmium
Who'd retired as primuspilus years before.
I knew the family too – would often visit.
Now Priscus' wife – for Priscus was his name –
Was quite a termagant, ambitious too,
Determined to take advantage of the chance
Presented by this superfluity of men;
Persuaded good Priscus to invite to dine
The officers of the staff and garrison,
To celebrate, he said, the agreement made
At our conference. And so it was I came.

Imagine then, my pleasure and surprise
When I saw this same officer in the room –
The one whom we had commented on before –
He had that presence which draws men to him.
I greeted him and introduced myself,
And Diocles turned – for that is who it was –
Did I not say?

              We talked of this and that,
And then the conversation turned to sport,
I said the hunting hereabouts was good.
'D'you hunt the boar?' excitedly he asked.
'Indeed, we do.' A great smile lit his face.
There and then a hunt for boar was planned;
I said I would make arrangements the next day.
He was the kind of man you are glad to please.
Instinctively you knew, he had deeper thoughts
Than you would ever have, but you felt no shame.
When he spoke to you alone he made you feel,
He thought of only you and shared with you
The wealth of his innumerable ideas.

Before we dined, Priscus' children came
And joined us as we stood around and talked.
Prisca, the eldest, ensured the guests were helped
To the many delicacies which the servants brought,
That no cup was empty, no guest left alone.
That must have been the first time that they met;
He must have noticed her, for next I knew,
Good Priscus' house was full of marriage talk.
No one was sure how long the Army would stay

DIOCLETIAN

So the formalities were completed fast,
Enquiries made of prospects, dowry agreed,
The augurs consulted, the marriage day was fixed.

And as by now, with the hunting of the boar,
We became quite friendly, so seemed natural
That I should be invited to be the auspex.
Auspex? At a wedding – You do not know?
I forgot – the Caucasian rites are different.
At a Roman wedding, the marriage cannot start
Until the sacrifice to the gods is made,
And the auspex has inspected the beast's entrails,
And guaranteed the auspices are good,
And the future for the pair is favourable.
A family friend is asked to do this task;
I knew them both; it seemed appropriate.
I can't remember what I saw that day,
But know I would have concentrated more,
Had I realised it was an Emperor's fate
That the entrails of the sacrifice revealed.

But the revelation was for me, the bride;
I had known her since the day she had been born,
Had seen her grow, and lose her puppy fat,
Become a serious and fine-featured girl.
But now in all her finery she stood,
Her saffron coloured cloak and matching shoes,
Her hair prepared just as the vestals do,
And over all the flaming orange veil,
Topped with a wreath of sweetest marjoram
With myrtle and orange blossom intertwined,
Her inner happiness outshone her clothes
Bursting forth affecting all who saw
Making all feel better by the sight.

I found the auspices were favourable;
The marriage could proceed – and silence then
And Diocles and Prisca made their vows:
Ubi tu Gaius, ego Gaia

The rest is for me a blur, a joyful blur.
Shouts of Feliciter! and much happy laughter
The wine flowed and people merry made

PREPARATION

And danced and sung the daylight hours away.

Then time to take the bride to her new home.
With flutes and torches leading all the way,
I remember the hymn of Hymen beautifully sung,
And bawdy ballads, lots of smiles and laughing,
The nuptial torch, and crowds of lookers-on
And throwing nuts and sweetmeats to the kids
Who thronged about the route, and so we came.

I remember the threshold of his borrowed house
And Diocles standing there to greet his bride
He carried her across, and bedlam then
As we entered and everyone milled around.
I think I can recall the formal offering
To her of fire and water by the groom.
Since then I have been to many marriages,
And memory increasingly plays tricks on one.
I think the distaff and the spindle came;
I know I saw her taken to her room,
And remember how the bridesmaid closed the door.
I remember Diocles standing waiting there,
As we sang the formal songs and bawdy ones;
And into her he went, our singing grew,
And gradually we left, I remember, happily singing,
Late in the evening in Sirmium...

                          But look!
That light towards the left, that's surely new,
Another camp fire in the night, another raid.
Turn out the guard. The Imperial Guard turn out!"

— * —

        Diocles to young Prisca came,
        Tenderly confident.
        He saw her lying there prepared,
        Tentative and radiant.

        With gentleness, he spoke her name,
        As if it were an experiment,
        And saying it, he knew he cared,
        No longer was he hesitant.

DIOCLETIAN

Carefully untied her belt,
Felt her warmth and her consent,
And in her trust, he sensed that peace,
Within which he would rest content.

Whatever hand he might be dealt,
Or dire hazards might be sent,
He felt his confidence increase,
With her, he felt omnipotent.

Durostorum: Legionary Commander AD 277
aet. 33

A tortoise approaches the military way,
   No wind – the grass hardly a quiver.
Warm on the road in the late glow of the day,
   No one to be seen right down to the river.

There's a murmur of bees; the crickets' noisy call.
   Ants are carefully climbing the vine.
Warmth, calm, contentment over all,
   Peace for the moment on the frontier line.

A heron floats lazily towards the north
   Where the marshes stretch for mile on mile.
A lizard watches what the ants bring forth,
   The tortoise takes another step meanwhile.

A trumpet sounds —

The regular tramp of military men,
   And the busy noise of mighty Rome
Has taken control once again.
   The Eleventh Claudia are coming home.

The soldiers sing as soldiers do,
   The time to pass, the miles to eat,
Some songs are old and others new
   But there must be a regular beat.

      Left — Left — Left, Right, Left.

      Sin — Sin I had a good job and I sinn'd
      For — I — disobeyed the Lex
      — Next — Next — What can I do next?
      SIN — Sin I had a good job and I sinn'd...

PREPARATION

>So fifteen more steps are taken
>To reach Durostorum fort,
>"We'll show girls we've forsaken;
>To treat us as they ought."

The dust settles slowly at the close of another day,
The tortoise finally crosses the military way.

— * —

Standing where the tortoise crossed the military way,
We can see the commanders cantering up the hill,
Relaxing at the end of a satisfactory day,
And now dinner together, nothing more demanding.
The nearer of the two is the commander of the Eleventh Claudia,
Alert, looking around him, while the other speaks;
And the other, thinner and taller, with a patrician air
Is Constantius Chlorus, commander of the Prima Italica.

"I like these combined exercises. It does the men good –
Showing off their skills to each other and learn something too.
And I think the tribesmen are impressed, whatever they say,
To see the legionaries parade along the line –
A change from the limitani, the frontier force.
Half the time they can't remember whether they're farmers or soldiers.
You are new in the job, Diocles, but mark my words:
When you've been here a year you'll appreciate the chance of a change
Which these shows of force allow you."

                "There's Durostorum,
A warm bath and then dinner, and we can continue then
To sort out the world, Constantius. But first a bath."

— * —

Now the dinner is cleared, the commanders and their staff at ease,
Enough wine's flowed, it is the critical hour
When intellects have been encouraged, but not too taxed.
Diocles is sitting there listening. He looks ready to pounce.
It's as if he was starving and new ideas are sustenance.
The wine is passed round. Diocles turns to his guest
And asks him his view on the present circumstances.

"The present circumstances, Diocles?
Thin, sir, thin – stretched extremely thin.

DIOCLETIAN

My fort, as you know, is named for sixty ships –
Sextaginta Prista – but how many are left?
Hardly a score – not enough to patrol the river.
No wonder the barbarians break through again and again.

"And take our two legions…" Constantius was well away now.
"Fine men indeed but half of them away on detachment
Fighting other wars in the Orient – We have both served there;
We know their need but here we are stretched too thin.
Thin, sir. Too thin…" And his voice, it died away.

"And now they are made to dig…"

                                                "What is that you say?"

"In Italy the legionaries, wherever the land is untilled
Are made to tend the vines and plant the corn.
It's one thing for the frontier forces to work the fields;
They hold their land by right. It goes with the job.
But our job as legionaries is to show the power of Rome,
Knock sense into Goths – but digging ditches – Charming!"

Then another angry voice: "The Army's might
Sets Emperors up. It just as well can set them down."

"Gentlemen!" Diocles had heard enough. "It's true
We need more soldiers. We are indeed stretched thin.
But soldiers need food as you all appreciate.
For this reason the noble Emperor Probus intends
To have all abandoned land in cultivation.
More food means more recruits and more men here."

And when the Commander spoke with such certainty,
There were none there so foolhardy as to challenge him.
All that remained was the need to say goodnight
And leave their Commander to his private thoughts.

And left alone he thought:

                              They do not know
How difficult it is to create things that are new.
I must prepare myself for the task that's to come.
I have the will. I can contribute.
All that is intractable I must contemplate.
Great Jove. I pray let me not be too late.

PREPARATION

— ✽ —

At dawn next day the Prima Italica parade
Ready to set out on their journey back to their base
Constantius thanks his host and bids farewell
"Come visit us soon. We are closer to you than Rome!
And the hunting around us is good."

                                   "Hunting you say?"

"Some of the best hunting of wild boar in Moesia."

Diocles stopped as he turned – "Hunting, you say ?
Boar hunting is a pastime I love dear."
The surprised Constantius has at once to fix the day.

The Prima Italica march down the military way
And the tortoise wakes to face another day.

Dux Moesiae

AD 282
aet. 38

[You know, I am not sure that I trust this man.
He says he serves on the staff of the Praetorian Prefect.
He knows I can check the fact, so it is probably true.
But I have never met him before – He's too familiar,
And indiscreet as well, but by design,
For here we are, among my personal staff
Relaxing in the mess, after a hard days work.
This persistent gadfly keeps on dropping hints
And watching carefully how everyone responds.

Heaven knows that life is difficult enough,
Without having to cope with an agent provocateur.
Since I was named the Dux Moesiae
There has hardly been a quiet day on the front,
Besides the pressing need, to supervise
The settling of the Bastarnae in Thrace.
The Emperor Probus agreed to let them in,
At their request, for they were pressed themselves
By other barbarian tribes from further north.

I know he chose me as I had shown some flare
For administration, while at Durostorum
In command of the Eleventh Claudia where I held

DIOCLETIAN

These same Bastarnae back, north of the river.
And now this gadfly seeks to know how far
I am committed to the Emperor Probus
And the feelings of my staff and if they are loyal
To the Emperor Probus and, what is more, to me!

If Marcus Aurelius Carus, Praetorian Prefect,
Is taking the trouble to sound his colleagues and peers,
This strongly suggests disaffection exists in high places,
So possibly now is the time to take soundings as well.
Now let us, gadfly, talk of this and that,
So I may be more clear, and you confused,
For now is the time one should be circumspect.
When Emperors change, we soldiers gain – or fall.]

"Dux Diocles, I appreciate this chance
Of conferring quietly with you privately.
From what your officers said in the mess just now
It seems the Emperor's restoration plan –
Using the soldiers to reclaim the fields
Which the barbarian incursions have laid waste –
Does not meet with much enthusiasm here..."

"Our men are busy here holding the line.
They have no extra time to dig, good sir,
[What is his name? Gaius Gadfly?] but understand
I comprehend the Emperor's need for land –
This land yields crops. These crops provide the wealth
Which can be taxed and that provides our pay
And all our sustenance." [Take that, Gadfly,
And may it neutralise the foolish words
Spoken by my officers in the mess.]

"And Dux Diocles, I heard it said that Probus..."

[Plain Probus now!] "The Emperor, Sir, you mean."

"Indeed! The Emperor Probus did himself
Declare that soon there'd be no need for men
To stand to arms and in the army fight.
The consequence of defeating all our foes
Logically must put soldiers out of work..."

PREPARATION

[So, he wants to snare me with that odd remark
The Emperor made in jest.] "Be clear, good sir,
[What *is* his name?] that we are fully booked
From now till end of time, holding the line.
Peace there may be elsewhere in the realm,
But here there's constant fighting to be done.
Whatever may occur in other places,
I must stay here – Barbarians to the north
And the Bastarnae in Thrace are quite enough
To keep me and my legions fully occupied."

[So Master Gadfly read there what you will:
Either, I am loyal to Probus and will hold
The Moesian front intact whatever should happen,
Or, Carus rising, I will stand aside
With my two legions, and will wait and see.]

"Now, tell me sir, what news of General Carus?
I served with him in Egypt heretofore,
Under the Emperor, before he came to power."

"That I know, for Carus speaks of you
With great respect, as one who contemplates
All aspects of a problem, before you act."

[That, Sir Gadfly, is as broad a hint,
As I have heard, since you came here to stay.
Indeed, I will all aspects contemplate,
But how confident is Carus of his cause?
Probus before was popular with the troops
For he ensured they all were well equipped,
Was recognised as fair.]

        "What feel the troops
Now that the peace has come?"

        "They do object,
Diocles, to all this agricultural work.
I appreciate the reasons for the drive
By the Emperor to reclaim the untilled land,
But, sooner or later, reaction will set in.
Praetorian Prefect Carus has advised
The Emperor, more than once, to moderate
His enthusiasm for the country life."

DIOCLETIAN

["Country life"!, so that is how they speak
Of the Emperor Probus, among his senior staff.
It's changed a lot since when I served with him.
I think that 'wait and see' is best for me.
But let me leave this Gadfly with the thought
That I have two strong legions at my call.]

"I hope that now you are here, you will spare the time
To see the legions stationed on this front.
What? You have to leave so soon – a shame –
I would have valued your opinion
Of both the legions' battle readiness.
Please give the Praetorian Prefect my regards.
I am looking forward to entertaining him
When he next comes. The hunting here is good."

So when the nameless gadfly left next day
He noted the legions on the Moesian front
Were loyal to the Dux Diocles, that he would wait
The outcome of any move which Carus made.
He also noted the hunting of the boar was good
In the scrubland and the forests thereabout.

The Boar Hunt

AD 282
aet. 38

A man stands there alone with spear in hand,
Absolutely still, watching the wood.
The sound of hounds from further up the hill,
And the shouts of men, casting to and fro,
For the quarry which they had followed since first light,
Is somewhere in the thicket gone to earth.
The warmth of the morning sun – hardly a breeze,
So quiet that the man can hear the grass move back
From where it had been trodden under foot.
A beetle moves with care between the stalks
Of the nearest lupin flowering on the hill,
And two flies settle on the upper leaves;
Intently the man is watching the wood ahead.

Lower down the hill his servant stands,
Bridle in hand, calming his master's horse.
From where he is, the hillside is clear to see –

PREPARATION

The watcher, still, standing there alone,
The hounds, their handlers and the mounted men,
Searching the further side of the scrub oak wood,
For the track they had been following now seemed lost
And all their sweat and labour useless waste.

Deep in the thicket, the old boar also watched,
His mean red eyes peering through the grass,
Tired from being chased; everywhere the threatening stench
Of the excited dogs and the noisy huntsmen's sweat
Unsettled him and he backed further in.
He heard the men calling the hounds to heel,
And sensed that threatening order now prevailed.
Danger, fearful danger from that side,
But lower down the wood, hardly a sound.
Something was there – the old boar felt the call,
Seductive, tinged with fear, completely right –
He had not survived all those many years
To lord it over all the beasts, a very king,
Among the hillside thickets and the scrub
Without that instinct sent from a special god
Which in a crisis told him where to turn –
He felt it now. He turned to the lower edge
To see what called him with such certainty.

Meanwhile higher up the hill, a change,
There is now an anxious tone to the huntsmen's call:

"Where's Dux Diocles? Isn't he with you?"

"I thought he'd joined your group. He's not with us.
He must have turned aside. He often does.
He'll be all right. He's got his man with him."

"I wish he'd let us know when he decides
To wander off alone during a hunt.
Shouldn't we hold back the hounds awhile
Until we know precisely where he is?"

"Too late! The hounds are already in the wood.
I think Diocles knows what he's about,
He's a specialist in the hunting of the boar."

DIOCLETIAN

Everything is deadly quiet below the wood,
Diocles waits, watching the lower edge.
Further down, his servant also stands,
Too far off to be of any help,
But close enough to see and hear it all.
Great happenings have their need of witnesses.
The servant is a plain straightforward man,
Not given to great imaginings or thought,
But nonetheless he knows why he is there.
He sees it all with growing clarity,
As minute follows minute – must not forget –
He is chosen of the gods to be a witness.

With a shrill shriek like the trumpets' battle call
The Boar charged. Diocles turned to face,
For in spite of all his care the crafty boar
Had reached the thicket's edge without a sound
And now like a cataphract charged down the slope.
Diocles knelt, he just had time to jam
The spear's butt in the earth – the battle joined,
Man and beast, inextricably intertwined,
The spear's shaft snapped, the fangs, the teeth,
So close the dangerous bite, the froth, the stench,
Eye to eye they were, and then they glazed.
Man and boar covered in each other's blood
Under the morning sun – and neither moved.

The servant shouts – he is jolted back to life.
He runs towards his master, calling for help,
And reaching the bloody bodies, there is a stir.
"Get me out from under all this mess, good man.
This is too close to being a sacrifice!"

And the servant knows that which he has just seen –
A happening holy to the ancient gods,
A sacrifice – but he is a simple man,
He cannot explain the reason for what he saw,
But he knows, and will until his dying day,
He has witnessed something rare and holy there
On the hillside, under the early summer's sun.

Much joking and laughter, and a general air of relief –
Diocles somewhat washed from the brook nearby;

PREPARATION

The boar, the spearhead still in its bloody breast,
Is hoisted on two poles for all to see,
In triumph leads the procession back to town.
All wonder at the size of the ancient boar
And guess his weight and estimate his age.
And while they are doing this, a rider comes,
Salutes Diocles, "Sir, I bring you news."

"Out with it man. You've ridden far and fast.
You must be as impatient to report your news
As I to hear."

              "Dux Diocles, Sir,
I come Sirmium where Probus was.
He who was Emperor is no longer so.
Praetorian Prefect Carus has assumed the purple.
He had been away in Raetia collecting troops
For the coming war that is planned against the Persians.
The Raetian legions made him Emperor."

"And what of Probus, pray?"

              "He climbed a tower
To oversee the clearing of the land.
Some soldiers turned on him and cut him down,
Then all proclaimed great Carus Emperor."

Gone was the heady excitement of the hunt,
Some shivered and others turned and looked away.
Diocles, still smeared with blood of the boar, looked grim.
"We'll speak more of this anon."

              And then he turned
And as a joke, wryly he spoke these words:

"I'm always killing boars but the other man
Is the one who grasps the chance to enjoy the meat."

But the servant, standing close, remembered all
He had seen that day, and then he understood–
He had seen an ancient boar, a very king,
He had seen his power passed on in sacrifice,
He had seen the annointing of an Emperor.
Not now maybe, but with certainty, he knew
His master would, in time, be Lord of All.

DIOCLETIAN

— ✳ —

"From the very day on which I heard the news
That Probus had been butchered in his tower,
Increasingly I was drawn within the web
Of imperial power of the new Emperor.
The gadfly must have said I would remain,
With my two legions, quietly on one side,
When General Carus challenged for the purple.
But the gods in their wisdom decided otherwise;
My loyalty was never put to the final test.
Probus fell to his infuriated troops,
Before Carus had the time to stake his claim.
With Probus dead, Carus gained his end,
And the luxury of avenging Probus' death.
But with no insurrection, it was not clear
Who were Carus' friends, and who his foes.
So Carus gathered his known supporters close,
But also all of those whom he wished to watch –
And which was I, when I came to court,
Neither he nor I were absolutely sure.

First came the summons from the Emperor
Calling for me to come to Sirmium.
I felt alone, as I entered camp,
Shorn of my legions, very much alone.
But Carus welcomed me as an ancient friend,
Offered me command of the Protector corps,
The same which I had joined ten years before,
Which placed me close to watch and to be watched;
Then, as if to emphasise his trust,
And reinforce the new established bonds,
Named me a suffect consul for the year.
Such a little time there was to make the change
From being one of many in support,
To being one of the few essential ones
Close to the centre of imperial power."

Everywhere was bustle at the camp;
Daily, contingents came for the campaign,
Which Carus planned against the Persian power,

PREPARATION

Weak and divided since Sapor was dead.
He named his elder son Carinus, Caesar,
To take command of the empire in the West,
Meanwhile with Numerian, his younger son,
He prepared the army for the Persian war.

THE PERSIAN CAMPAIGN: OPPORTUNITY
in which preparation leads to opportunity to fulfil that which has been foretold

Beyond the River

AD 283
aet. 39

"I don't like it. I don't like it at all.
Here we are camped beyond the river,
Beyond the limit set by the oracle,
The limit natural to the power of Rome."

"Oh. I don't know. It is not as bad as that.
The boys did well. Seleucia and Ctesiphon
Fell to us almost without a blow.
Our mighty army, with Carus in the lead,
Without hindrance marched between the rivers;
Hardly a fight, almost a summer jaunt."

"But we have come too far! I feel that it's so,
And if you look at the way our chiefs behave,
I think the generals too lack confidence.
They scowl at one another, hardly speak,
Except to pass the order of the day.
And rumour says the Emperor is ill.
What will become of us if he should die,
Deserted beyond the Tigris, leaderless?"

"You worry far too much, my friend, I'm sure.
It is not for us, mere common legionaries,
To second guess the plans of the command.
We are from the Eleventh Claudia, don't forget;

DIOCLETIAN

Our chief, or should I say, our former chief,
The Dux Diocles will look after us.
He's a careful man – no harm will come to him –
Nor to us, if we stick close to him."

In the turmoil of their fears they are not alone –
As vital blood is with an ill infected,
Gradually the weakness spreads from limb to limb,
Till none stands firm; the body's whole collapses –
So it was Rome's army teetered on the brink
Of that natural sphere allotted by the Gods,
And on the brink of losing all its form:
They had lost their confidence, they had lost their way,
The campaign between the rivers had passed with ease,
Hardly enough of Persians stayed to fight.
Ctesiphon had fallen – no battle call –
The mansions, palaces, the treasuries and stores
Lay unprotected, open, no one there,
No one to challenge the Imperial Power of Rome.
Carus, encouraged by his Praetorian Prefect,
Pushed on and further on seeking the Persians,
But none was there. They crossed the Tigris river.
The land was sparse and dry. The cold wind blew.
They were alone in Asia's vast expanse.

— * —

When Maximian entered, Diocles was alone
Contemplating the course of the campaign,
How different from the great Aurelian's war –
Then all was clear, the enemy fiercely fought,
With loyal comrades, Palmyra was overcome
And Imperial Rome's authority restored.
Now the uneasy Persians slipped away,
Occupied as they were in internecine strife,
Drawing Carus and his army on and on,
With none to fight, none to negotiate.
The frustrated Emperor encroached upon by time,
Sought glory in his final last campaign,
An easy prey for younger crafty men,
Ambitious for themselves, not for the state,
And such a man was this Praetorian Prefect…

THE PERSIAN CAMPAIGN: OPPORTUNITY

"Ah! Greetings, Maximian. You're a man I'm glad to see.
Here I've been sitting depressed with dreary thoughts
Full of frustration and lack of confidence..."

"Lack of confidence? That's surely not like you."

"The lack's not in myself..."

                    "Thank God for that!
Would have been another certainty come unstuck!"

"The confidence I lack is in the general staff
Surrounding the Emperor. He has such little time
To achieve what he wants for his family and for Rome.
And there are those as aware of this as I,
Who take advantage and give unwise advice,
Encourage him to reach, further and further
Into the uncharted, unknown..."

                    "Oh come, Diocles,
To me at least it is clear. It is time I spoke.
I have soldiered with you for all these many years,
I owe you much. I was the one you called
To join you in the dawn outside Palmyra,
That hectic chase after the fleeing Queen.
Because of you Aurelian noticed me.
I owe you much, and now you are going to listen.

Firstly that lack of confidence: there's one
And only one in whom you have your doubts;
That is our Praetorian Prefect, and those doubts
Are magnified because he is Father-in-law
Unto Caesar Numerian, the Emperor's son.
We are all aware Numerian's a cultured lad,
A talented poet but hardly a governor,
Easily directed – as easily deposed.

Secondly there's time, or rather lack of it,
For the years encroach on you as on any man.
You need the time for policies to mature.
Not months, nor years, but decades are required
For all those plans breeding in your brain
To have a chance of seeing light..."

DIOCLETIAN

                      "Enough!
Maximian, enough. I've never heard you talk
Like this before…"

                             "…And never will again,
But bear with me. This strange and empty place,
This lowering day, sunless, overcast,
Disembodies me and therefore feeling thus,
I can speak as in the real world I never would.
You can be Emperor, if you seize the chance.
That you desire it, that is widely known,
The jest you made after hunting boar
Is oft repeated – "Others enjoy the meat" –
Make sure Diocles, it is not so again.
Time is too short and there is much to do
And you are the man, Diocles, now is the hour.
And thirdly…"

                      "Maximian, wait. The day draws dark
Strangely so. A taper at this hour?
Ho, there! Bring a taper. We need a light."
[This he said as much from embarrassment
At having his closest thoughts put into words.
You need not light to hear the truth.]

                        "And third,
Diocles, you are an observant thinking man.
You must have realised there is a further reason
For lacking trust in our Praetorian Prefect.
There is the significance of his very name:
This man you fear is Lucius Arrius Aper."

[A is for Aper. Aper the boar.
It is as wild a beast as ever you saw.]

The taper flickered. The two men with their thoughts
Stared at the lonely light, alone in the tent
As the day darkened. The wind moaned through the camp.

Outside the sentry shivered and hugged himself
The wind was rising. Darker and darker yet.
Then an uneasy murmur of thunder to the south.
Darker yet. The sentry put out his hand,
His fingers he could not see – full stretched, were lost.

THE PERSIAN CAMPAIGN: OPPORTUNITY

The thunder again, closer the warning call,
But warning of what? The sentry shivered again.
A thunderous clap, a mighty flash, then quiet –
All was quiet throughout the frightened camp,
And then a cry of utter desolation,
A single cry – "The Emperor is dead".

Diocles came through the door. "Turn out the guard!"
Shouts in the darkness elsewhere in the camp,
Other generals shouting, calling their men to arms,
Torches trying to pierce the unnatural gloom.
Before order could be achieved or fears resolved,
A conflagration which restored the day;
All now could see the Emperor's pavilion
Which had become his very funeral pyre.

— * —

Two days passed before the council met,
Two days full of quest and conference –
How had the Emperor met his fiery end?
What happened on that fated ill-lit day?
Who now should lead the legions, demoralised,
Aimless and lost, in the land beyond the river?
Arrius Aper, the Praetorian Prefect, held
All in check, controlling the Emperor's guards,
Directing his body-servants and his slaves,
Thus Carus instructed before he took to bed,
Stricken down by a malady, most strange and rare,
Which mystified his doctors, dismayed his men.
None of the council therefore could discover
Precisely what had happened on that day –
Some said that Carus had at last succumbed from his fever,
And others thought that a thunderbolt had struck
Punishing the presumptious Emperor, who had ignored
The repeated warnings of the oracle.
But how explain the sudden conflagration?
Was it a thunderbolt, or the slaves distressed,
Who in their grief had fired the Emperor's tent?
Certain it was that among the charred remains.
No one could find a hint of evidence,
Of what had happened on that darkest day.

DIOCLETIAN

Diocles pondered long what he should do,
Maximian's words sharp printed on his mind,
The army leaderless, beyond the bounds
Of Rome's imperial sway, without an aim;
Numerian a talented youth, but born to peace,
Not made of stuff from which are leaders formed;
The devious Aper maintained a strict control
Of the Imperial household so that none could know
How Carus died or how Numerian lived;
That Numerian lived was sure, but Aper watched
The every action of his son-in-law.

Diocles sensed, after due conference,
That most of his peers, uncertain of the facts
Of Carus' death, conscious the legions stood
Far from home deep in the Persian land;
Held that regard for proper authority
Outweighed the advantage of new leadership.
He sensed his brother officers would prefer
Numerian, the rightful son and heir,
Even with devious Aper father-in-law,
Than risking a coup all these miles from Rome.

So when the council met, business was brisk.
The Generals, Senators and Companions
Were gathered together in a new pavilion.
As Numerian approached, the trumpets called,
Greeting him Augustus, the shout went forth
Echoing back from off the dry hillside
On that drear and empty plain in furthest Asia.

Thoughts

AD 284
aet. 40

Diocles thought – plenty of time for thought
During the long withdrawal through Mesopotamia.
At first Numerian, with Aper's encouragement,
Considered emulating Alexander.
The common soldiers soon put paid to that;
They made it clear they felt too far from home,
Fearful of the fated oracle and the omens,
They insisted that the only way was north.

THE PERSIAN CAMPAIGN: OPPORTUNITY

But the withdrawal had been a lingering affair;
No Persian authority to negotiate,
In spite of waiting throughout the summer months
For plenipotentiaries from the King of Kings,
That terms might be discussed to end the war.

Diocles thought the army's slow withdrawal
Was in part because Numerian feared his brother,
And foresaw the bitter rivalry to come,
When he assumed his share of imperial power.
And meanwhile Aper – what was the part he played
In the direction of the youthful Emperor?
It was certain he had encouraged Numerian to extend
Himself and the army further than was wise.
Had he done this that then he might seize power?
Certain it was, that Aper now controlled
All access to the Emperor, as before
When his father had lain sick. But sick of what?
No one had seen him. No one knew for sure
How the Emperor Carus died – now what of his son?

Diocles thought Aper must not succeed,
Though Numerian not necessarily survive.
Neither man is suited for the task
Of ruling the Empire in these fractious times.
How to allow Aper sufficient rope,
So Aper could achieve his end, in such a way
That prevented him from taking of the fruit?
And so Diocles thought, and thought, and thought.

Loyal Advice AD 284
aet. 40

"My Lord?"

       "Good Diocles. I need advice."

"I am at your service, sir."

          "I am concerned
That I, as Emperor, make a contribution
To the safe and seemly ruling of the realm.
It is by chance we are here alone…"

DIOCLETIAN

                [By chance!
If you knew how long this meeting took to fix,
Careful timing and cunning subterfuge...]

"...You have a reputation for deep thought
About the affairs of imperial governance.
Since my father's death I have been alone
For long hours, time to contemplate
On chance that created me my father's son,
Made him Emperor, and placed me by him,
When he by the thunderbolt..."

                [Get on. Get on.
Get to the point. We have little time alone.
My planning put to risk by rhetoric!]

"Sir. How can I help?"

                "In short, tell me
What I should do to make a lasting mark
Upon the Empire and its government."

"Sir. There is one act, a contribution,
Which you, the Emperor Numerian, can make.
It may to you seem lacking in import,
Irrelevant to the present needs of state,
But when your father noble Carus died,
The council was concerned, above all else,
That proper due authority prevail.
Too many coups have spoiled the due process
Of legal transfer of imperial power.
With loyalty and unanimous relief,
As Carus' son, you were proclaimed our lord.
Numerian, you have as yet no son,
It is essential therefore that you do ensure
The council has the authority, if you should die –
I put it bluntly, Sir, as time is short –"

[Short indeed, there are steps outside the tent.]

"...Authority to name the successor to yourself
With the proper transfer of imperial power."

"Indeed I see the point. It shall be done,

THE PERSIAN CAMPAIGN: OPPORTUNITY

Ratified when the council next shall meet.
For this loyal advice, Diocles, heartfelt thanks –
Here comes the Praetorian Prefect. Why the scowl,
Good Arrius Aper. Here we are all friends.
Life is far too short for surliness."

[Too short indeed for all that must be done,
For all the plans breeding in my brain,
But time enough for the giving of loyal advice,
Loyal to the Empire and its governance.]

Vigilance

AD 284
aet. 40

"I don't like it. I don't like it at all.
It's not natural – moving us around.
The Emperor's guard should be permanent,
Not drawn from the legionary ranks as if by lot,
And then dismissed, just when you understand
The special duties of the imperial guard."

"Oh. I don't know. It is not as bad as that.
We are from the Eleventh Claudia. We are as good
As anyone including the Protector corps.
By this scheme it's certain we have a chance to see
The Emperor in person, and what is more important,
To be seen by him and by the top brass too.
You never know, they may remember us!
That can't be bad, and could be profitable."

"But have you noticed how the Praetorian Prefect
Watches all the while the Emperor,
And never lets others be with him alone?
It's not natural I tell you. The Emperor
Is a friendly enough young man, but seems to me
He's more a prisoner that a potentate."

"You may be right. Others worry too.
Our decanus was saying, only the other night,
That the centurion had been cross-questioning him –
You know the one who's on Diocles' staff –
He had asked our decanus for details of the guard,
Where every man was posted and if alone..."

DIOCLETIAN

"And don't you see? Even the officers
Of the Protectors – They are kept in the dark."

"Indeed this Centurion, so our decanus said,
Seemed to suggest that Aper was up to no good.
He said that Dux Diocles was concerned,
Disliked the constant changing of the guard,
And hoped that all good men be vigilant."

"Vigilant. That's the word. Vigilant.
We must watch that Aper. We must be vigilant."

The Emperor Passes

AD 284
aet. 40

"Look here they come! What a wondrous sight.
I am glad you said that we could watch them pass,
The mighty army of the Emperor."

"They may look fine to you, to your young eyes,
But certain I have seen better in my time
When the great Aurelian…"

"What, him again?
Uncle, you always talk of the good old days
When men were men, and boys were merely boys."

"But it was so. When Aurelian came this way,
His army sparkled in its heady pride
Straining at the leash, ever eager to find
The foulest enemies of Imperial Rome.
Now look at these, but shadows of those men
Who marched against the Queen Zenobia.
No scouts ahead of the army in these days.
I know they are in Bithynia, safe and sound,
But regulations specify that scouts
Should go ahead to check that all is well,
Even when in the Empire's safest parts.
Look at this vanguard, a sorry scruffy lot,
The horses of the cavalry not groomed,
The infantry, ill-kempt, with rusted arms.
I don't know what the army's coming to."

THE PERSIAN CAMPAIGN: OPPORTUNITY

"Where's the Emperor? You promised that we'd see him.
Is that him that's next coming up the road?"

"He should be next, if they keep the order still
Which the army used to follow on the march,
But I cannot see him mounted on his horse.
Your young eyes are sharper, what do you see?"

"Certainly no Emperor, Uncle, riding high,
Baggage I see, then it's not clear what's next,
Could it be a litter carried by horses,
The kind which noble ladies often use?
But why?"

        "A litter, yes, and with a guard,
I think it is the Emperor, he must be sick,
But something's wrong about the imperial escort.
They are not the Protectors; they are plain legionaries.
Ah, here they come, the Protectors, that's more like it,
Well turned out, that's Diocles at their head.
He was a young centurion in the tenth
When I was in Arrabona years ago.
I may have told you."

        "Yes. Indeed you have!
Let us wait and see more of the army pass."

"No, we must back to home to keep good watch
You never know what scavengers there are
When the army is on the march, all is then at risk."

"But you made sure our stock and our provisions
Were safely stowed away in the summer steading.
What is now at risk?"

        "Not much more, I trust,
But I was taught in the Quartermaster's stores
Two things, the first was good intelligence;
Maintain this all the time. Why do you think
We moved the stock and stores, just when we did?
And the second is: Always double check!
So off we go."

DIOCLETIAN

>"The Army was good to see.
Even if they were not as smart as in the days of old.
I am sorry the Emperor is sick."

>"I am sorry too.
In fact I did not like what I saw at all.
The Emperor all confined so none could see –
Without the Protectors, he seemed a prisoner.
The Empire has surely come to a pretty pass
When you cannot see your Emperor riding by."

The Trap Snaps Shut   AD 284
                               aet. 40

The November day was drawing to its close
At the staging post on the old Imperial Road
Two days march from Nicomedia.
The advance guard of the army had passed through
Three days since, and now the Emperor came
Escorted by the Eleventh Claudia,
Close carried in a litter to protect
His infected eyes from all the dirt and dust.
Beside the litter, the Praetorian Prefect rode
With his personal escort of Praetorians.
The litter halted at the door of the Emperor's tent,
His chamberlains drawing closely all around,
Almost as if they were suffocating him.

The light was fading fast, the torches lit,
The cooking there by the camp fires, all relaxed,
The sounds of men preparing for the night,
Shouts in the dusk as the imperial guard was changed.

"I don't like it. I don't like it at all.
We haven't seen him for at least five whole days,
They say he's sick, troubled with his eyes –
I would have trouble with my eyes, cooped up in there –
None of the boys have seen him, I have checked around.
How can you guard one who is invisible?"

"Oh. I don't know. It is not as bad as that.
When we asked the Praetorian Prefect how he was,
He assured us, all the Emperor needs is rest.

THE PERSIAN CAMPAIGN: OPPORTUNITY

Arrius Aper sees him every day,
And conveys his orders to the army staff.
If the poor man has bad eyes, it is right he should rest."

"But that's just it. Aper sees the Emperor,
But are we sure the Emperor can see Aper?
His eyesight is bad for sure, but just how bad
I think we need to know. I smell a rat –
Perhaps it is something more! There *is* a smell –
A distinct imperial smell. We need to watch,
Watch that Aper, we must be vigilant."

"But how be vigilant if you cannot see
The object you have been told to vigilise?"

"Ay. That is a point. We needs must burglarise,
The better that we both may vigilise.
You are much nearer to the door of the tent than me.
Be quick, have a look. All's quiet and no one stirs.
What can you see?"

"Nothing. He is not here!
Look in the litter. It's there – close to you.
Wh — what — what can you see?"

"It is dark in here.
Now I can. My god. He is cold and how he stares.
Quick let me out. I need to breath the air."

The two legionaries, staring, stood transfixed,
Neither spoke nor moved, utterly undone.
Silence throughout the camp, they were alone
With their knowledge that Numerian was dead.

They moved, whispered and then they quietly called
Their decanus – told him; he sent one of them
To seek their centurion for this was far too great
A matter for mere common legionaries.
The centurion like so many of his rank
Had heard the warning from Diocles' men:
"Be vigilant. Aper should be watched."
But here was he, commander of the guard,
With his imperial charge, betrayed, alone and dead.
And what of Aper, the man who should be watched,

DIOCLETIAN

Aper who said Numerian needed rest,
Aper who had made sure he got that rest,
Aper. Arrius Aper. Where is Aper?

The men from the Eleventh Claudia approached his tent,
Shouting for Aper, calling for his death,
A brief struggle, and Aper was in chains.
He had staked his claim, he had played, and all was lost.

The breathless runner came to Diocles' tent:
"The Emperor is dead. Aper apprehended..."

There was much more but Diocles hardly heard,
[The trap has snapped shut, but now care is required,
The utmost care if we are to achieve our goal.]
"Have the General Officers and the Council told.
Ensure that Arrius Aper is held safe
So he can appear before the imperial council.
Let there be no arbitrary exercise of vengeance.
Go see to it. Let the rule of law prevail."

The Boar is Slain

20 NOVEMBER
AD 284
aet. 40

Now see a plain outside Nicomedia,
The regiments of the army, rank on rank,
The legions with their wall of coloured shields,
Each proudly showing their distinctive battle signs,
The heavy horse, the Moorish javelin men,
Federates and mercenaries, all on dress parade.

Five days have passed since Aper was arrested,
Since Numerian was discovered in the litter, dead.
Five busy days of careful consultation.
The council, mindful of Numerian's wish
That proper transfer of imperial power
Should be observed, and that the council had
Authority to name the successor to Numerian,
And mindful also that the common soldiers
Too often would arbitrarily make their choice,
And having made the Emperor, him unmake,
The council therefore called to the parade
Men from all the arms and every regiment.

THE PERSIAN CAMPAIGN: OPPORTUNITY

On the tribunal were the council members
High above the parade for all to see,
Before the Eagles and the dragon standards
Displaying the full emblazoned Army power.
Afranius Hannibalianus began to speak,
As senior general in the Orient,
Declaiming from a carefully written script...

"I don't like it, waiting around like this."

"Silence in the ranks. Pay attention to the General."

"Oh. I don't know. There's all that money to come."

"Silence! Another word and no gold for you.
You may think you're smart electing an Emperor
But don't forget, I'm here when they're all gone!"

"...Your council with authority in it vested,
With approval of the Senate's members present,
With concurrence of all general officers,
Of the ever victorious mighty Army of Rome,
Shocked by the treacherous murder of your Emperor,
Have prayed to the Gods, consulted the oracles,
Searching with earnest diligence for the man,
Best suited to succeed to the great and onerous task
Of leading the Roman state in peace and war;
Our unanimous choice which we now present to you:
Gaius Valerius Diocles, Imperator Augustus."

Augustus! Augustus! Augustus! the Army roared,
Their weapons reverberating on their shields.
They approved the choice, welcomed the donative,
This proved the Emperor was an Army man.

Bassus, the senior member of the senate present,
Turned to Diocles, standing for all to see,
Placed the purple cloak upon his shoulders,
The purple cloak, the sign of imperial power.

[I have done it! I, Diocles, have finally done it!
Not the end, but the beginning. It all starts here.
This Emperor making must be well remembered...]

"Bring forth the prisoner, Lucius Arrius Aper.

DIOCLETIAN

You ask how the noble Numerian met his death?
This is the man who contrived the deadly deed.
The Emperor was in his care, in his alone."

"Vengeance! Vengeance! Who will avenge Numerian?"

Diocles drew his sword, held it on high.
A hush throughout the ranks, all wait and watch.
The two men face each other, neither moves,
Then Aper drops his eyes, the sword descends.

A sigh from all as if they had held their breath,
Diocles, spattered with the dead man's blood:
"At last, at last I have killed my fated boar!"
The roar of the Army throbbing in his ears –
The old witch in Tungria; the dead boar's head
Grinning on the summer hillside in Moesia.
Diocles stared at his bloody hands and arms;
He wiped his sword on Arrius Aper's coat.

"Let the parade proceed as custom does dictate.
We must not delay. There is much work to do."

TO HAVE AND TO HOLD
in which Diocletian confirms his hold on imperial power and comprehends the problems facing his inheritance

Carinus Hears the News

ROME
late
AD 284

Carinus was waiting in Rome. He had waited long
For his brother's return that they might celebrate
The victories they had achieved in East and West.
Almost a year he had waited for Numerian,
But his brother showed no enthusiasm to return.
He had dallied in Syria and now in Bithynia,
While Carinus had wasted a precious year in Rome.
Wasted a year? Hardly – for he had enjoyed
The many diversions that the city had to offer
To all young men and particularly to an Emperor,
Public and private games, feasting all night.
Now in the dog days of the year, no news,
Nothing from Asia for more than one whole month.

It was after dark when the courier posted in,
Drooping with tiredness, wet through with sweat and rain,
Thrust with little ceremony into the Presence,
He kneels and shaking, proffers the despatch.
Impatiently Carinus breaks the wafer, reads,
And cries with rage. All that he had feared was there.

One by one his advisors and staff come in,
Warned of the late night messenger from the East.
The despatch the Emperor passes to his Prefect,
Turns to the messenger: "Tell me yourself, my man,

DIOCLETIAN

What you heard yourself of this dread act."

"My Lord, Your brother Numerian is surely dead,
And dead for many days before I left,
Riding post-haste to bring the sorry news.
He had suffered from infection of his eyes,
And so was carried close within a litter.
Praetorian Prefect Aper attended him,
With such concern so none could him disturb.
Slowly the army wended its weary way…

[He was enjoying the importance of the hour,
Holding the attention of an Emperor.]

…In short, Sir, the stink, if I might use the word,
Became so evident – was remarked by everyone –
That the common soldiers demanded to see their Lord,
And that they did, in spite of Prefect Aper;
They found him dead, cold and stinking dead,
They had humped a corpse all through Bithynia."

"And then what?"

                "My Lord, Aper was arrested.
My general sent for me, told me to mount
And bring this news to you without delay.
And that I did. That is all I know, My Lord."

Two days on, Carinus' council sits,
Discussing how best the Emperor should respond.
Only a year ago all seemed set fair,
Carinus twice triumphant in the West,
Both in Britain and against the German nations,
But then ill news from out the Orient:
Carus, target of a deadly thunderbolt,
And now Numerian dead of an eye disease,
Confined in his litter, left alone to rot.
How best could Carinus now regain that power,
Which Great Jove seemed determined to withhold.

A knocking at the gate, a brief delay,
And another dusty courier is escorted in.

"News, My Lord, I bring news of great import."

"Out with it, Man."

TO HAVE AND TO HOLD

"The Army of the East
Has proclaimed Augustus, Valerius Diocles.
He was named by the council of the Army in the field
And confirmed with acclamation by all ranks."

"When did all this happen?"

"Ten days since.
The crossing of the narrow sea was swift;
I determined to be first. Five days had passed
After your brother was discovered, lying dead,
And Aper had been arrested, held in chains."

"Diocles commanded the Protectors. Did no one suspect,
He'd had a hand in the killing of my brother?"

"If they did, they held their peace, and Aper too,
His peace is more profound than any man's."

"How's that?

"As the roars of acclamation fade,
The unfortunate Aper is dragged out for all to see,
Shown to the ranks by the new-made Emperor.
'This is the guilty man,' Diocles shouts,
And drives his sword between neck and shoulder bone.
Anointed with Aper's blood, he stands aloft,
Avenger of Numerian, and Lord of All."

"My brother's avenger? My brother's usurper more like.
What know we of this Diocles? Who's served with him?..."

At last they had hard facts with which to work,
No longer speculation, they now could plan.
They felt relieved, however bleak it looked,
As Carinus took advice to counteract
The new found threat from this upstart in the East.

"I have served with him, My Lord. I know him well,
Or as well as anyone can know that man.
He thinks deep and long before he decides to act,
He keeps his counsel close unto himself,
Seldom acts on impulse, most by design,
So the sudden killing of Aper, for all to see,
Seems strangely out of Diocles' character,
Unless..."

DIOCLETIAN

"Unless? Perhaps it was designed.
He blotted out both killer and all trace
Of incriminating conspiracy, most foul.
It seems this Diocles is a cunning man.
We must ensure he doesn't infect the rest,
Who elsewhere hold authority in the realm.
Let us list the Governors, Correctors and Praeses.
We are sure of all the West – what's there between?
Constantius holds Dalmatia. I think he's sound..."

"But, Sir, I know that under Aurelian,
He was a Protector with this Diocles.
They may be close..."

"Who knows Constantius well?
Whom can we send to hold him to our cause,
And keep us posted of his moods and thoughts.
There is no doubt that Dalmatia is critical,
Lying as it does there between our powers.
And what of..."

[Carinus impulsively pressed on
He preferred to act rather than contemplate.]

"And what of Sabrinus Julianus? Where does he stand?
As Corrector Venetiae he is placed strategically
Commanding the way into Pannonia.
I like the man. I think he's reliable.
Find me someone who's sound to send to him.
Now let us consider those under Diocles' sway,
He holds the provinces of the East, but not much more,
A third of all the Army at the most.
That is the message we must spread abroad:
Augustus only in name. Lord of a third!"

His courtiers laughed, encouraged by his brave words.
But before he could say any more, shouting outside,
"An urgent message for the Emperor. Make way. Make way."

"Sir. I come from Julianus in Venetia."

"What news from friend Julianus do you bring?"

"News indeed, but not news from a friend.
My Lord, Julianus has assumed the purple.

TO HAVE AND TO HOLD

As soon as he heard of Lord Numerian's death,
He proclaimed himself Augustus there and then.
I heard it said that all the Pannonian legions
Have declared for Julianus and are moving south."

Suddenly all the waiting is at an end
Carinus felt relief. He is free to act.
Gone are the sybaritic days of Rome,
Let all in heady action be forgot.

"Get me my horse. We are away within the hour.
I will teach this Julianus to put on airs
And when he is done, it'll be Diocles' turn."

Recording the Likeness

NICOMEDIA
AD 284
aet. 40

"Sir. Please keep still. I have a job to do"
[What is it about this man that is hard to catch?
The light is good enough – we are facing south;
It may be December but only an hour after noon.
In fact he is keeping still – it's his looks that change,
Reflecting the rapid activity of a busy mind,
Which bring small alterations to the tilt of his head,
Or the gleam of his eye, not easily obvious,
Except to one whose trained to art like me.]

Diocletian responds, he calls his body servant,
Instructs him that he is free for no one else
Until the picture-making is complete,
He settles himself, adopts his imperial glare,
Holds it for a moment until his thoughts awake.

[It's clearer now that the answers are to hand
Or some, at least. Moesia is sound
But no surprise, that's my old hunting ground,
The rest of their two legions ready to march.
I am glad Constantius has responded well.
I was not completely sure of him myself;
The position he holds in Dalmatia is critical.
He has no legions but there are auxiliaries.
The formula he suggests seems to me fair enough,

DIOCLETIAN

The auxiliary commanders are free to declare for me,
He will not discourage them, and when they have
That will isolate Dalmatia in the south.
Carinus meanwhile is tied up in the north –
A lucky chance, with some encouragement,
Julianus claiming the purple when he did.
The stores for the campaign are coming to hand
But even in midwinter it's taking far too long.
We must speed that up for when the Spring is here
There will be Carinus or the other man to fight.]

"That is better, Sir. I have your likeness now.
A few more minutes, the sketch will be complete."
[Complete? How can I show the essence of this man?
His outward appearance is clear: of medium height,
Of medium build, no sign of great excess,
Neat beard, moustache, of conventional Illyrian cut,
With high brow, eyes deep set – it is the eyes that show
The difference between this man and all the rest.
They say that the eyes are the window to the soul
And this man's soul is complexity itself.
When other men believe they see the whole,
This man sees it inside, under, out,
In such a way, that others comprehend
Much more completely, and are glad for that.]

"I am glad you are nearly done. There is much to do,
But the making of my likeness is part of it.
To all the provinces the likeness must be sent
As formal confirmation of my reign.
The mints will need the likeness for the coins –
So ensure you make me clearly who I am!"
[Better likeness, finer minted coins,
More glorious banners carried by the legions
Each with my likeness confirms the stability
Of Gaius Valerius Diocletian Augustus' reign.
Sounds good – All this goes to reinforce
That essential sense of imperial stability.
And the pomp and ceremony of my imperial court
All contributes. Augustus is apart,
He stands above, he is no common man –

TO HAVE AND TO HOLD

Augustus so why not Augusta as my wife?
I told her that many lesser wives had been
Honoured by lesser rulers through the years.
But she said no. She knew Diocles,
But found it strange to embrace a living god.
But there's Valeria, a sweet and serious child
Growing yet more beautiful with every day.
Prisca loves her and I would myself
If the gods allowed me time to be alone
With these two women of my family.
But there is work to do...]

"My Lord, it is done.
The original will be ready in the morning at the first hour
For your approval, and then the copiers
Can go to work, so the world may know their Lord."

Rededication

After years of war my lord came home,
But what a change was this.
Gone for ever the man on a quest,
The seeker I knew before,
Who needed me.

Now my lord is the Lord of Imperial Rome,
Too mighty for a kiss,
Too busy with affairs for time to rest,
Our spirits to restore
And contented be.

But the gods are kinder than mortals be.
We have a wondrous gift,
Valeria, the certain sign of our love,
Will constantly be here
To remind us both.

She recalls those days, before we could see
The coming of the rift,
When together we called on the gods above
To bless our life so dear,
And plighted our troth.

DIOCLETIAN

But my lord is Lord of Imperial Rome,
Valeria the wondrous gift,
I will live my life for this sign of our love
Seeking what I knew before –
For they need me.

Diocletian's Dream

AD 285
aet. 41

I dreamed, last night, of a man with a loaf of bread,
An honest man, such as you might meet
In the course of ordinary business, any day.
But he had an anxious look as he grasped his bread,
In doing this, I was drawn to him;
He needed me and I had need of him.

I stretched forth my arms to the furthest bounds,
Trying to hold his world in my embrace.
I stretched and stretched, my sinews strained and cracked,
I felt the edges with my finger tips,
But could not hold the world, it slipped away.
The man's despairing look remained with me;
He needed me and I had need of him.

Far below me, I could see the man
Standing alone, holding his loaf of bread.
Beside me, behold, two others regarding me,
As strangers do visiting a foreign land.
The elder had an air of authority;
I knew he understood about the man,
Who needed me and how I needed him.

The other stranger, young, thickset and strong,
Stood ready to fulfil the high commands
That his companion's fertile mind might make.
With awe, I felt the power of these two men
Who comprehended all that they beheld
Spread out below, the busy Roman world,
The towns, the farms, the soldiers on the march.
And I heard a voice: "Take note. Remember well
All that you see, for you see it through our eyes,

TO HAVE AND TO HOLD

How everything has an effect upon an other,
And to this puzzle you will add your piece,
But now is the only time you will see the whole.
Remember well the men with the loaf of bread,
The one who has need of you, as you of him."

— * —

Now it is afternoon, I am alone;
The morning's business with the council done,
Companions, staff and counsellors dismissed,
And as I rest, I have time to contemplate.

What meant the dream, what meant the gods' commands,
For without a doubt they were gods in truth I met,
Who gave to me this vision of the world,
Its interlocking problems once displayed,
Just once, for there wouldn't be a second chance.
The all-powerful Jove had granted me this gift,
Supported by his helper, Hercules.
They gave no names but I knew with certainty,
For by their presence, gods reveal themselves.

They said "Remember well!" but alas it's gone,
The clarity with which I saw the world
And all the problems I have now to solve.
Great Jove help me recall, comprehend this world,
And help prevent it slipping right away.
Help me save the man with the loaf of bread.
I dedicate, confirming this request,
My family and my reign to you, Great Jove.

Suddenly I feel a surge of certainty.
At the centre of the puzzle is the man with the loaf of bread.
He is all men in the Empire, of every rank,
Slave or free, all have need of me,
And I of them, for me they justify,
They are the reason for my very being.
The loaf of bread is his sustenance.
To live a man must eat, for if he starve,
What use is living, be he free or slave.

DIOCLETIAN

And through your eyes, Great Jove, what saw you there?
Beside the man, the town, the countryside,
With trading in the town, farming outside,
All to gain the wherewithal for bread,
Money being used and elsewhere barter too,
And also close to hand, roads and ships,
Temples and fine buildings, frontier forts,
The army and religion provide a shield
Against the foes of this world and the next.

These we saw on a plane beside the man,
And on another plane encircling it
Evil influences eager to despoil:
Plague, and untilled fields everywhere,
Foul atheism tainting ancient faiths,
Currency losing value, the townsmen flee
Away from the towns and responsibility,
The expanse of Empire, distance without end,
And ever the Barbarian clamouring at the gate.

This was the puzzle which I had to solve:
Two planes, the first was ordinary common life,
And on the second, influences malign
Ruining the life of the man with the loaf of bread.
But in my dream I'd seen yet another plane,
Ill-defined but certainly of great import,
The gods had said that I would add my piece
And there it was for me to comprehend.
Help me, Great Jove, help me to clearly see,
What I must do to save the falling world.

>Briefly and clearly then the third plane's seen:

>Imperial stability above all else,
>With a long reign and no sudden coups;
>The Emperor therefore must be held in awe,
>God-like names and ceremonial.

>With this stability all barbarian hordes
>Are firmly kept outside the Empire's gates,
>With as large an army and as deep defence
>As may be required to maintain the peace.

TO HAVE AND TO HOLD

The utter tyranny of distance will be reduced,
By seeking partners to undertake the task.
For just as Jove has need of Hercules,
So must Imperial power be shared and spread.

For this stability there will be a price,
With peace, the countryman will tend the land,
The trader safely travel throughout the realm,
And of this wealth a legal tax be raised.

The third plane is seen… it already fades.

"Ho. There! Send me a scribe. I must record…"
But no. It is gone. Great Jove, stay at my side,
Help me to help the man with the loaf of bread.

The Honest Man's Song

A man must eat, that's sure,
And if he has a wife,
Doubtless they'll need more
To sustain them in this life.

He must need to have a trade
So he can earn his bread,
Or dig with fork and spade,
To ensure that he is fed.

He'll need a house to live,
Roads to get about,
Town walls that safety give,
And keep barbarians out.

He should worship ancient gods,
Who keep him safe and sound,
For they reduce the odds
Of danger all around.

The dangers are real enough;
Barbarians and the plague
Are but two which make life tough,
And there other threats more vague.

DIOCLETIAN

Inflation everywhere,
Gods held in disrespect,
Rich citizens disappear
So their duties they neglect.

Emperors come and go;
We're ready to be led
By someone who will know
How to keep us fed.

For a man must eat, that's sure,
He needs to earn his bread,
He needs to feel secure,
That's why he must be led.

Highway Intelligence

AD 285
aet. 41

The sound of the horse's hooves faded away.
The resthouse above Lychnidus was empty now,
Nothing to do until the next one came,
Now was the time to rest and speculate.
What meant this rush of couriers on the road,
In winter time when all should be at peace?

In calmer times travellers stopped to rest
And admire the view across the mountain lake.
The imperial way through Macedonia
Had long since ceased to be a military way,
Now that the frontier was established further north.
But the road remained the quickest way for news
From out the East to reach the City of Rome.
The humble resthouse keeper always knew
When the mighty of the Empire were astir,
By the number of couriers and how long they stayed.

"Another one and he hardly touched his food."

His wife was annoyed but she must understand the facts.
"You should appreciate these are important men
Who carry the heavy burden of government."

TO HAVE AND TO HOLD

"But heavy burdens require the strongest back
And that, to my mind, means a proper meal."

"You do not understand the half of it.
Do you think we are only here to give them food
And provide fresh mounts?"

        "That is all it seems to me."

"No. We are here to understand the whole.
We live in stirring times which necessitates
All good men to know what is afoot."

"And what do you know?

        "Enough. I know enough.
The middle ranking couriers are the best
For the giving of reliable intelligence."

"Intelligence?!"

        "Indeed. Intelligence.
You do not understand this world of men…
Now I have lost my train of thought… Ah. Yes.
The keen beginners do not stop to talk;
The senior officers of the service shun
Humble men like me, but those between
Like to pass an hour in company
Showing their importance by telling what they know."

"And what do they know?"

        "That he who was Diocles
Is now addressed as Augustus Diocletian
And he looks the part, a very proper Lord –
All is formality – no back slapping there.
The couriers approach him with respect and awe.
The other one is different, the one in Rome,
Carinus is friendly, especially to the women I'm told,
But he has gone north to fight, I know not who,
But certain is, he fights."

DIOCLETIAN

"So he is not in Rome?
Our courier could have stayed to break his fast.
It'll be many days before he finds his man."

"Diocletian sits in Nicomedia,
He sends his couriers to every governor.
I guess he does not speak of Carinus, well,
And probably promises there will be no change.
(You remember when the new inspector came?
He swore the service would be as before,
No change in fees or charges, but then behold
When we had relaxed, he turned all upside down.)
I expect Diocletian will be just the same.
But they say he's a thinking man with authority;
The gods know that we have need of a thinking man,"

"I hope whoever wins will govern well,
For that means many messengers, many meals,
And we get paid for meals, eaten or not."

The Business of High Politics   AD 285
aet. 41

"What I need is a bath, and then a meal."
Those were my thoughts as I handed in my bag,
But it was not to be. The chief had other plans,
So there I was standing outside his door
Waiting to be summoned, tired and saddle-sore.
I was a courier then, an agens in rebus,
The Master of Office was my superior –
Was a new post then with an ambitious man in charge.
We imperial couriers were given many tasks
As well as simply carrying messages.

This was a case in point. I had brought the despatch
From the headquarters of the Emperor Carinus, north of Verona.
He had just defeated Julianus and the Pannonian legions;
That was what the report I had carried, was all about,
And being important I had pressed myself,
And hence the pressing need for a good hot bath!

Just as I began to feel extremely cold
As my sweat dried – it was an early day in Spring –

TO HAVE AND TO HOLD

The Master of Office finally called me in.
He asked me about the battle Carinus had won,
But I sensed that that was not his real concern.
The Master questioned about Carinus' staff,
Who held what, who did the actual work,
And what they did when relaxing in the mess.
I had to admit that as a junior courier,
I hardly mixed with the Emperor's senior staff.
And then he turned on me with a piercing look:
"You are an agens in rebus, are you not?
Res, rebus, what does it mean do you think?"
I must have stuttered something, but he went on,
"Res – business. Everything is your business.
Whenever you travel, wherever you may go,
You must learn, mark and inwardly digest.
And that is what you are immediately going to do."

So there and then I became a practitioner
Of the applied science of imperial politics.
The Master made it clear with winks and nods
That what he spoke of came from the very top,
But I must be discreet and not disclose
Any of the matter discussed between us two.
"You are a likely lad, handsome and friendly too;
That is one reason for assigning you this task.
You are also intelligent…"

                        [This, he said,
I must admit, more as an afterthought!]

"…You must return to Verona without delay,
Or wherever Carinus' headquarters now may be.
You will attach yourself to the staff, and there remain
Making yourself useful and acceptable.
Now tell me of the Emperor Carinus, what do they say?"

I remember saying he was very popular,
A man who greeted all as bosom friends.

"But more friendly," the Master went on, "with those endowed
By nature to be great bosom friends with him!
He has a leaning for the fairer sex.
No one is fooled by those coins which he has produced,

DIOCLETIAN

Those which do honour to his noble wife;
She keeps an eye on him, but still he strays.
Now this is where you help our master's cause:
You will discover Carinus' latest love
And who her husband or protector is,
Whom you'll ensure understands the state of play.
Then if he's incensed you will encourage him
By questions such as, what makes cuckolds rank?
Answer: the rank of he who makes the cuckold.
And similar happy jests which will inflame
The sensitive conscience of the unhappy man.
But if he be complacent you should observe
That the lady will despise him when it is done
Because he accepted the imperial competitor.

To those who rest assured their loved one's loyal
You will observe her looks have saved her yet,
But that she's saved his chance of advancement too;
Promotion rests in the bed of the Emperor.
You will not cease until all married men
Spend all their time watching the Emperor.
And if they are single, you will indicate
That the Emperor despises their state of singleness,
So they too will grow to hate their Lord.
Do all of this with jokes and jests and hints
And you will be worth a legion in this war
That our Emperor Diocletian undertakes."

I remember feeling flattered, excited too,
That I had been selected for this task;
I think I felt disturbed by what I'd heard;
I know I felt I still required a bath –
And that I had – and soaking there I thought –
This is business – This is high politics!

The Gods See All   AD 285
                         aet. 41

From high above the northern frontier river,
Among monumental clouds, cloud on cloud,
The gods observe the ant-like activity of men,
Caught up below, the busy struggling crowd.

TO HAVE AND TO HOLD

Along the river bank the military road,
Studded with forts and observation towers,
From the northern side the barbarian nations watch
The civil conflict of the Roman powers.

In all this hectic rush a pattern forms,
Following the river Margus from the south
The Asian legions with utmost care advance,
While others join from the frontier river's mouth.

Look to the west, an army from Pannonia
Is closing rapidly with the firm intent
Of stopping these two armies coming together,
Averting the threat their masséd ranks present.

Laid out below is Viminacium,
The legionary base, critical to the campaign;
Here the Margus and the frontier river meet,
Whoever holds this will a clear advantage gain.

Will the gods intervene in this struggle of mortal men?
Will they stamp on the ant heap and finish the civil war?
Whatever the cunning stratagems of men,
The gods alone decide what lies in store.

The Battle of Viminacium

AD 285
aet. 41

The Emperor stood on the bank above the river,
He could see from there his army, all deployed;
Close to, the right wing on the military road
By the broad river marking the northern limit
Of the Empire, whose very future lay at risk.

"Whose very future lay at risk?" – Not so.
His future was at risk. Whatever passed
The Roman World would be there in the morning,
But he, Diocletian, could not be so sure.

He briefly wondered what the barbarians thought,
Watching from the northern bank the battle lines,
How Romans in civil discord destroyed themselves.
So much to do, so much to be set to right,

DIOCLETIAN

But first the need that his authority
Be accepted in the West as in the East.

Looking towards the south, he could just see
The legionary cavalry drawn up on the left.
They, combined with archers, had to hold that flank
Where the land rose among the scrubwood and the thorn,
Doubtless good for hunting of wild boar,
But difficult going for the cavalry in formation.

Before him the legions in battle readiness stood.
He saw the Eagles, the familiar dragon flags,
All the standards of the Army of the East;
There too the legions from Moesia,
Worth the time which waiting had consumed.
With this time he'd have met Carinus further west,
But then been outnumbered more than even now.

Behind him the fort of Viminacium,
The home of the Seventh Claudia, there in line.
Along the rear the road stretched to the south.
Far ahead stood Margum, in the morning mist,
Were the Margus and the northern river join;
There his rival Carinus slept last night.

Sun-up comes late in the early days of spring,
The mist upon the river is slow to clear.
The soldiers of the legions have been in line
Since those small hours when all are shades of grey,
Both sides determined that their battle line
Should be in place before the first attack,
For all is common in a civil war
Of military training, traditions and strategy.
The advantage rests in the feeling of the men,
How long they'll accept brother killing brother.

"My life has come to this. The final test.
Months of planning, the preparations made,
All has been done which a single man can do.
May the gods confirm that I was born to rule,
That I will have the time to complete my task.
Now all is set. The battle lines prepared,
The men harangued, encouraged for the fight,

TO HAVE AND TO HOLD

Well rested and provisioned, all deployed
As well as the field of battle will allow.

My mind runs on reviewing all that's done.
The right is well protected by the river,
The centre manned with fresh Moesian troops,
And the reserve, with friend Maximian in command.
I'm glad to have him there for he is loyal,
And god knows now is the time for loyalty.
But I'm still concerned about the southern flank,
I have placed the cavalry and the archers there,
But how will they perform in the broken ground,
But that same ground will hold up Carinus' men,
But – I think I worry yet again – all is set.
Let the gods decide if I am to rule the world."

From his vantage point the Emperor saw the battle joined:
The familiar coloured shields, the battle flags,
The horns which called the advance, the shout of war,
As the enemy, the Pannonian legions pressed the front.
The wedge was formed but before it could drive home
The Moesian veterans countered, cut it off.
The hard fought battle in the centre's evenly poised,
Quiet here on the right, how goes it in the south?

"Sir, General Hannibalianus sends his respects,
He asks for support to counter the enemy thrust,
The federate Gothic horsemen prove too strong,
They are expert in the use of the terrain."

In the rush and noise of battle all is obscure,
No time to act. Too far away to help.

And then another courier posted in:
"Sir, the flank has been turned, our men withdraw
To prevent the Gothic horsemen riding wild
Behind our lines. We still maintain our front
But have sore need of help from the reserve."

But what reserve? Outnumbered at the start;
All spare men committed to the fight
To hold the centre and the Pannonian thrust.
Now real danger that the flank be turned,

DIOCLETIAN

The line of retreat to Viminacium cut,
And the world of Diocletian at an end.

And then a miracle —

                The Western onslaught ceased,
Not in a moment, but more gradually
The attack lost force; the defence found time to breathe.
Shouting was heard in the Western Army's ranks:
"The Emperor is dead. Long live the Emperor."

Diocletian still maintained his vantage point,
Uncertain what this happening might mean.
Wary of a trap, he continued to keep his guard.

A trumpet call, a shout, a flag of truce,
A party approaches on the military road.

"My Lord – the Emperor Carinus is no more,
Murdered by a member of his retinue
At the height of battle. We are leaderless.
We ask your mercy, we acknowledge you our Lord,
The rightful master of the Roman world."

Much more was said, formal and otherwise,
To establish what had actually transpired,
Personal and general business to be done,
Appointments to be made, Armies combined.

Later that day the Emperor Diocletian,
As unchallenged ruler, received Carinus' staff,
Accepted their submission, save for him
Who had disloyally spilt imperial blood.
When told he was a jealous husband, wronged,
Had killed Carinus to revenge his wife,
The Emperor was adamant – no reprieve.

Later still on that great and memorable day,
The members of the court relaxed, recalled the events,
Discussed together all they had seen and heard:
"Our man won, but the gods know it was close."

Another said, "It shows virtue is rewarded,
Our man concentrates, no bits of fluff
Would divert our Diocletian from his aim."

TO HAVE AND TO HOLD

"It is sure the gods have been with us today.
Our man respects the gods and they help him,
It is wonderful how the gods have helped our man."

The Master of Office said that he agreed:
"Indeed, the gods help them that help themselves."

FULFILLING THE DREAM
in which Diocletian begins the task of saving the Empire and enrols Maximian as his helper

The Emperor at Work

SIRMIUM
AD 285
aet. 41

At break of day they had had the Emperor's call
To be prepared when all the rest had gone
After the morning formal salutations,
To attend on him to talk of high finance.
They now were waiting in his anteroom,
Each apprehensive of the new man's ways.

It is passing dangerous to be a friend of kings,
Its power exciting but the risks immense,
All knew their fortune rested on his whim,
For men so often change when they gain power.
It did not matter they had all known Diocles,
For that was another time, that chrysalis
Had been transformed to Augustus Diocletian,
Lord of the Roman world, a man to fear.

Full of contrast standing in the dawn,
The seven men there at their Lord's command,
The Praetorian Prefect hid his uncertainty –
He had served Carinus before the civil war.
That the Emperor retained him in the selfsame role
All thought a sign of excellent moderation,
But Aristobulus knew it had been a deal
Struck before the battle on the Margus.

DIOCLETIAN

So here he was, appearing to be in power,
Concerned of what his new master thought of faith,
What he thought of loyalty, and how long he would survive.

The old Praefectus Annonae standing close
Listened with patience, born of experience.
His department filled the army's many needs,
An older version of that quartermaster,
Who had lectured young Diocles in Arrabona
On the art of planning adequate military supply.

Chatting together two veterans apart,
Hannibalianus and friend Maximian,
Who had served together in many varied campaigns,
But even Maximian now was on his guard;
He had known the Emperor, since as a raw recruit
He had joined at Arrabona years ago;
But former messmates should not ever presume
Familiar friendship in this transformed state.

In contrast, two grey men stood just apart,
Confident in their well worn competence.
They were the masters of the two bureaux,
Which controlled the finances of the Emperor.
The Sacrae Largitiones concerned itself
With mines and mints and public revenues.
The Res Privata dealt with the privy purse
Of the Empire's greatest proprietor, the Emperor.

Alone there stood the man of many names,
His fine breeding evident from his very stance.
Where most men seldom had more names than three,
The noble senator Bassus used all his six,
And expected others to use them when addressing him,
A senior member of the Senate, very aware of it.
He had been named consul with the Emperor,
Which showed to those traditionalists in the Senate
The respect with which this new man held them all.

The doors are opened, the Emperor awaits,
Now begins the business of the day.

— ✻ —

FULFILLING THE DREAM

"Here I am. Diocles turned Diocletian. Different.
And here they come.
They all have changed even though they look the same."

[Acknowledge each salutation formally.
Must not forget the ritual response.]

"Take good Maximian. Known him since he joined.
I recommended him for his first promotion.
Served with him in the East, in Gaul, and on the Danube.
Fierce. Tough. Loyal. And now shit scared."

[Another salutation – That I almost missed.]

"And Hannibalianus – they came in together.
Comfortable now in each others company?
It was not always so – after his daughter died,
He half blamed Maximian for not taking more care of her,
And took their babe into his own family."

[Salutations, again – and again.]

"Now Maximian has a fine new wife and children,
But wants his daughter back again, I hear.
Both good men. We need good men.
And Aristobulus is another good man.
You don't become Praetorian Prefect if you're a cypher.
He's looking decidedly circumspect – not surprising really.
He knows he is not one of the club – one of the clique.
But we are running an Empire now –
Good men in short supply."

[Salutation. My mind is wandering. I *did* miss one.]

"And Bassus of the many names.
I am not comfortable with Senators and all their breeding.
But the Senate cannot be utterly ignored,
But it must not be kowtowed to too.
There is only *one* Emperor.
But Bassus is a competent man and keen.
Maybe he can help me with Rome and the Senate."

[More salutations. I seem to be acknowledging them in my sleep.
When will they stop so we can get on with the business?]

DIOCLETIAN

— ✻ —

And they do finish, and the business does commence.
The Master of Office lists the business of the day,
The Emperor sits on the dais before an apse,
The members of the Council waiting to be called upon.
By protocol, it's first the Emperor speaks:

"I wish to consider the question of revenues.
This is the basic problem which we have to solve.
The Empire is beset by foes wherever you look.
In Sirmium we feel the pressure every day,
The innumerable barbarian tribes accumulate
Against the thin wall which our gallant troops
Hold tenuously together against the threatening flood...

[I know this sounds grandiose but needs must be,
An Emperor is expected to smoothly speechify]

"...but 'Protectores' need 'pecunia' for sure,

[And here a sycophantic titter round the hall]

"We will require the army to be expanded,
For by tradition the strategy of imperial defence
Has been based upon a powerful mobile force,
Led by the Emperor himself, wherever required,
But the Emperor himself cannot be expected to lead
In every nook and cranny of this vast domain,
So I propose we should defend in depth
On all our frontiers simultaneously.
If we can hold the barbarians in check,
Then the fields within the Empire can be tilled,
And peasants, tilling fields, can pay their rents,
And landlords have the wealth to pay the tax,
Which we require to keep the army strong.
Pray give me your advice, how we can make
The Roman Empire, sound and rich once more."

"My Lord," Aristobulus it was spoke first,
"You speak of paying tax, but pay with what?
Money has lost its value, year on year,
Gold and silver have been hid away,
And barter is now the means of all exchange,

FULFILLING THE DREAM

Except for the small transactions near at home.
My Praefectus Annonae I am sure can speak to this..."

"Indeed it is true, we take our stores in kind,
And pay all ranks in multiples of daily rations,
No cash for us, save only the 'stipendium'
Which is now but nominal, and the donative
Which you, Noble Sir, and your forebears give
On entering your reign..."

          "We need a system, then,"
The Emperor interrupts, "so our men can be supplied,
Without the country being ruined where the armies operate.
Arbitrary requisitions will not be tolerated;
Due legal form must always be observed,
And all should know how much they must contribute."

[I sound like that quartermaster long ago:
'To seize your needs, without legal form, is a crime'.]

Aristobulus balked at this new idea.
"To know precisely what the army needs
Down to the final nail and bag of hay,
Is an undertaking, hard to contemplate,
And if you plan to add new legions too,
The problem multiplies."

          "Aristobulus,
How do you provision the existing units now?"

"My Lord, there is a requisition list,
And this is based upon the nominal roll
Which is adjusted according... but you know this."

"Indeed I do. But what I want to see
Is less of ruined fields... [I must not make
Aristobulus appear incompetent.
His cooperation is what the Empire needs.]
Praetorian Prefect, study with your staff,
Ways and means of legally drawing stores,
Throughout the realm for an army twice the size."

"Sir, It shall be done..." [...but god knows how!]

[Sooner or later I will get my way

DIOCLETIAN

I will have a survey made of every town,
And in each town – each field, each olive grove,
And in each house – a complete census taken.
Sooner or later... but – I think, not now,
Not with Aristobulus. He cannot see
How we must plan, if we are to survive.]

The Emperor turns to speak to the grey men
Who head his two financial offices.
"What is the present state of the imperial mints
How stand the plans for my new currency?"
[Everyone always admires a handsome coin
The outward sign of a Government's inner strength.]

The Head of Sacrae Largitiones speaks:
"My Lord, fine new designs have been prepared
For your consideration and I trust
For your approval but..."

                                      "Another snag?"

"My Lord, we have a problem with supply
Of sufficient precious metal for the mints.
You have requested higher quality alloy
With a higher ratio of silver or of gold
To the base metal used in recent times.
My office supports this change in policy.
Alas, there is not bullion in reserve –
And production of the mines inadequate –
Sufficient to sustain the new issue which we plan."

On hearing this, there is considerable concern,
Particularly among the soldiers in the council room.
Maximian expressed the general view:

                                    "My Lord,
It's essential, at least, to have the gold issue.
The opposing armies have begun to join together,
And all rejoice the civil war is done,
But with no customary donative – there will be hell!
So good gold coins are needed for the Peace."

[That is more like the friend Maximian I have known]

FULFILLING THE DREAM

The concurring nods and murmurs, all about,
Made Diocletian comprehend the strength
Of feeling, there, among his counsellors.
A bitter pill to swallow but it is a fact –
Soldiers don't fight for love; they must be paid.

After a pause the Emperor continued to speak:
"We will concentrate upon the aureus in gold.
Prepare for me a plan how to control
The content and the weight of every coin.
I suggest we clearly indicate the fact,
By incorporating signs in the design.
My coins, as well as looking good, must be
Well known for their reliable intrinsic worth."

"But from where can we get the gold?"

                                                     "Can we revive
The custom of cities giving golden crowns
To celebrate an Emperor's victory?
Look into this, I pray."

                        "What about the silver?"

"The silver issue will have to be held in abeyance,
Until such time as we have sufficient reserves.
We will continue with the denarius with its silver wash."

"But Sir, its worth declines from day to day."
The grey man prevaricates and seeks for time.
"May we review this problem, and propose
How revaluation of the existing coin,
May help to stabilise the market place?

[I think the Master of the Sacrae Largitiones
Speaks like a learned man but I suspect
We have a problem which'll take years to solve,
But I am determined eventually that we will.]
"Pray do that. And now we will leave finance
Not that it will leave us for long I think."

[Another rueful titter greets this line.]

"Master of Office what is next on the list?"

DIOCLETIAN

"My Lord, we have the question of..."

                                          ...and so
We will leave the Emperor, newly Lord of All,
With his council, struggling how the best to solve,
The innumerable interrelated problems of the state.

Rotten Money

In the golden days of yore,
The denarius bought more.
The cynic said it was ever thus,
The common man said: "Why the fuss?"

"Our brutish life is short,
For finance we care nought.
We just need cash for food
To survive this life so rude."

But advisers in high places,
With anonymous grey faces,
Advised their Emperor how
He could make more money now.

"The coin's real value's such,
Its silver is too much.
Reduce the silver so
Your coin will further go."

And this is what they did.
At first their act they hid,
Ten percent at first,
Until at last the worst.

By Gallienus' reign,
They hardly could maintain
The silver on the skin,
With copper all within.

Meanwhile they issued more,
Than they ever did before.
Base minting thus proceeded
For what the Empire needed.

FULFILLING THE DREAM

This excessive circulation
Caused intense inflation.
While army pay grew twice
Wheat a hundred times in price.

From plague so many die,
Workers in short supply,
So rates of pay increase,
Inflation would not cease.

Aurelian tried reform,
Two larger coins as norm
Copper with silver plate,
The radiate crown in state.

Briefly he held the line,
Their nominal value fine.
Aurelian tried in vain,
For prices drift again.

Ruin all men feared,
Gold had disappeared,
Levies in kind the norm,
So government could perform.

Then Diocletian came,
The Empire to reclaim.
First must solve this nub,
Rotten money, that's the rub.

He counted man and beast,
And lands the great and least,
Decided what it could bear,
Had budgets to make clear…

…So all knew the demands
Of the military commands,
And regularly paid in kind
Goods specifically assigned.

The currency, he too reformed,
But prices out performed.
He tried control by Edict,
With results you can predict.

DIOCLETIAN

In the golden days of yore
The denarius still bought more
The cynic said it was ever thus,
The common man said: "God help us!"

Jove finds his Hercules   Sirmium
AD 285
"Sir, the General Maximian awaits your pleasure."   *aet.* 41

"Have him come in, and see there is wine to hand.
Then leave us alone. Make sure we are not disturbed."
[I had not realised just how difficult it would be,
For an Emperor to find the time for private talk.]

"Maximian, my friend."

"My Lord, you asked for me."

"Come sit you here. Relax. No ceremony.
I wish for your advice, just you and me."
[How circumspect he is, as if he feared
The arbitrary consequence of my imperial whim –
And well he might. My every word is law.
The Emperor is the source of all political power.
Ceremonial and formalities emphasise my authority –
And this appeals to me! I am set apart.
But now I would speak to Maximian as a friend
In spite of these trappings of my imperial state.]

"My Lord?"

"I wandered. Maximian, come sit here.
I trust you are well and enjoying Sirmium,
And the chance to be with your family once again."

"Indeed, Sir, and I have seen more of Theodora,
These days, than at any time since she was born."

"She keeps well in Hannibalianus' house?"

"Indeed she does, with all the confidence
Of ten whole years, she is wonderful to see.
But you did not ask for me to hear of this –
I am at your command."

FULFILLING THE DREAM

"You have heard the news from Gaul?
What make you of it? It seems they are just as bad,
As when we served in Tungria, years ago."

"Those Bagaudae are peasant terrorists.
The only thing they understand is force.
Talking sweetly to them does no good.
It seems that the local troops are in disarray.
Across the Rhine the German nations watch
How to gain from the troubles of the Bagaudae.
I would take the sword to them – No questions asked.
That is the only way to deal with terrorists."

"Then we have the Sarmatians on the central front.
They are pressing the frontier guards continuously.
The civil war encouraged them the more.
How do I cope with them, Maximian,
And free Gaul of the Bagaudae as well?"

"The size of the Empire is the very devil.
I don't know how you can split yourself in two."

"But I can, Maximian, that is the trick, I can!"

"How so, My Lord?"

"With you, I can do the trick.
I want you to go to Gaul and clean it up.
You have said how it should be done, so go ahead.
We have worked well together through the years.
You were a very lion of strength at the Margus fight.
Remember the hectic ride to the Euphrates bank?
Getting lost in the Tungrian marshes? There has been much
Which we have done together. We will do more.
What say you, Maximian, will you work with me?"

"Sir, of course I will work for you. You know I will."

"Not *for* me – *with* me, Man! I need your help,
As the arm has need of the hand, as close as that!"

"I will. I will. I will start for Gaul tomorrow."

"Not quite as soon as that. We must prepare.
I wish you to be Caesar and my son.
Everyone then will feel the authority

DIOCLETIAN

Which you, as Caesar, take with you to Gaul.
Formal adoption will confirm your place
As second only in the hierarchy."

"I am your son. I am at your command."

This was the beginning of the partnership,
Which was to last for all of twenty years.
Two very different men, one all thought,
The other action raw and fierce but loyal,
Bound together as Jove and Hercules.

When Maximian returned to Eutropia later that night,
She asked, as wives will do, what passed that day.
It wasn't in Maximian's nature to be discreet,
The secret bubbled out, he told her all,
And she, as wives will do, said what she thought.

"So the fox has had the sense to hire a wolf.
You will make a likely team, but do take care,
Let not your fiercest acts on his behalf
Be blamed alone on you. You are a team,
Make sure you share the credit with the blame."

Maximian hardly heard the words she said,
He was exalting in his Caesar-ness.

The plan proceeds. Jove has his Hercules;
Imperial power is shared. Distance reduced,
So in every province authority prevails.
The Peace of Rome will return unto the land.

The Senators' View

ROME
JULY 285
aet. 41

"Greetings, Senator, I like this time the best,
When the warmth of the bath draws out these stubborn aches
And gradually you and your body feel young again."

"Ah. It is you, good Manlius, I wasn't sure
In all this steam. I thought I knew the voice."

"Indeed. Indeed. Thanks to this steam there's less
Than there was of Manlius earlier in the day!
Needs be sharp and fit in these uncertain times."

TO HAVE AND TO HOLD

"It is certainly so, with someone new in power,
We all must look again at where we stand,
Both as the Senate and individually."

"Yes. Where we stand? There is one certainty,
The public baths are not the place to stand
If your objective is to have a discreet discourse.
Instead I suggest we withdraw unto my place;
Come dine with me tonight. We shall have the chance
Of reviewing all the happenings of these days."

And so it was that later these two men,
Colleagues, friends and experienced senators,
Discussed together fortune's latest turn,
How the man they had hardly known a year ago
Was now the sole Augustus Diocletian,
And the house of Carus utterly undone.

"Tell me, Manlius, you are well informed.
What know you of this man who is now in charge?"

"His father was a freedman, so I have heard,
A scribe in the house of our colleague Anullinus,
Or, in his father's house, to be precise."

"So he has had some education, more than some,
And yet, he shows the Senate scant respect.
He has not asked the Senate to ratify
His assumption of the purple, and what is more
He dates his reign from the day an army chose
This plain Diocles and made him Emperor.
No reference to the Senate. None at all."

"Come Aelius, I don't think it is all black.
He writes that he will model all his acts
On the humane example of Marcus Aurelius.
At least that shows he has heard of Marcus' reign
And all that it represents. He is well advised.
His emissaries have clearly stated none shall lose
For loyally serving Carinus with competence,
That none shall lose solely on that account.
And note that Aristobulus has retained his post –
He's Praetorian Prefect; he is sound enough a man.
It seems significant too he chose our colleague

DIOCLETIAN

Lucius Bassus to be his fellow consul
And now has named him Prefect of the City.
That surely shows the Senate some respect."

"But what do you make of the fact that Diocletian
Has moved his court to Milan, so close to Rome,
Yet he won't come here as tradition does demand.
And now he's appointed another raw soldier Caesar,
Proclaimed him such in Milan and not in Rome.
Manlius, our status has more and more declined –
First we have legions commanded by equestrians,
Then provinces no longer reserved for Senators,
At least we kept the right to ratify
The appointment of the Emperor, the highest in the land.
Now that is gone. We are ignored in Rome."

"But think, Aelius, about the alternative.
When we had the letter telling of Carus' death,
Young Carinus rapidly went from bad to worse,
Lax at best of times, gone was restraint,
Dissolute chaos reigning everywhere.
No man safe nor his loving wife,
And what was worse, all our property
He promised to give unto the city mob.
This man at least has sworn to respect the law
If he does this and protects our property,
He is my man; he has my support."

"But Manlius, it seems passing strange to me,
To have a Roman Emperor who knows not Rome."

THE EXERCISE OF AUTHORITY
by Diocletian both directly and indirectly

One year on. Much done. So much to do.
One whole year since he had stood alone
Smeared with Aper's sacrificial blood,
The soldiers' roar ringing in his ears.

One year on, and what had he achieved?
He was still there; to rule, you must survive.
Carinus dead, all now acknowledged him
The sole Augustus, ruler of the world.

Maximian Caesar triumphed in the west,
The bandit Bagaudae in Gaul dispersed,
The German nations pushed back beyond the Rhine,
Raiders cleared from the narrow British sea.

Here on the Danube front, his arms succeed;
Sarmatians put to flight. All now is quiet.
Defensive works proceed along the front
So all within the Empire may live in peace.

Much done. Much still to do. Another year,
Time for all the interlocking tasks
Which must be solved if the Empire's to survive.
May the gods make sure that there is time enough.

Despatches

OCTOBER 285
to
JANUARY 286

The courier had ridden hard throughout the night
For the imperial despatches must not be delayed,

DIOCLETIAN

Now in Thrace he had lost the Eastern court,
At every stop he had heard they had moved again.
Wearily the courier turned his remount east
And forced the pace along the imperial road.

The court was moving east to winter quarters,
All were relaxed throughout the retinue.
Their show of force completed against the Sarmatians.
Even the Emperor himself seemed satisfied.
Thus they were when the courier came charging up,
"Make way. Urgent despatches from Caesar Maximian.
For my lord Diocletian Augustus. Show me the way."

The Master of Office received the exhausted man,
Checked that he had not ridden all the way,
That the despatches he carried had been relayed from Mainz,
So the courier had no further news to give.
He sent the man to get his food and rest,
And took the letters to the Emperor.

"To Lord Diocletian Augustus, etcetera, etcetera,
Greetings from Maximian Caesar unto his Father.

I write to advise you of a development,
Which I have in hand, but you should be aware
As you may hear of it from other tongues.
As part of the campaign pacifying Gaul,
We cleared the narrow sea of Saxon raiders,
Fixed the defensive system of forts again,
Named for the region, called the Saxon Shore.

In achieving this, I was ably helped,
By one Carausius, who knew those waters well,
Born a Menapian, brought up in a boat,
A good soldier too, he was useful in the war.

Imagine my fury when I heard the news,
That Carausius had succeeded to such effect,
That he always caught the raiders as they returned,
Never sailing south seeking their prey,
But always sailing home laden with loot.
Neither our treasury nor the citizens
Have received account of what had been recovered;

THE EXERCISE OF AUTHORITY

Carausius and his gang have kept the lot.
He has become the greatest raider of them all.

A great disappointment; the clearing of the sea
I considered the very first victory of your reign.
All is in hand. I have ordered Carausius' arrest.
Summary court martial is too good for him,
I will report to you as soon as I have his head.

From Maximian Caesar, accept my duty. Farewell."

— * —

A few days on, the court reached Nicomedia,
Diocletian decided to pass the winter there.
While others rest, the Emperor contemplates
All that needs be done, and waits for news.
Not knowing and knowing that he does not know,
Exhausts the mind. He calms himself and waits.

Another courier, another despatch, more news.

"To Lord Diocletian Augustus, etcetera, etcetera.
Greetings from Maximian Caesar unto his Father.

I have more to report on the vile Carausius.
The men I sent to arrest him were too slow.
Carausius slipped across the narrow sea,
He took the fleet with him. We have none,
Not even a coracle to fish for eels!

And what is worse, soldiers suborned with gold,
Illegally stolen from raiders' treasure trove,
Declared for Carausius, so he is inviolate
In the island of Britain just there across the sea.
I will report again when I know more.
I am devastated by this change of fate.

From Maximian Caesar, accept my duty. Farewell."

Diocletian considered carefully for a while,
Ignored the gnawing feeling of fearful doubt –
A fully fledged rising, and only a year had passed –
But Maximian devastated, would be no help
In undertaking the Herculean tasks

DIOCLETIAN

Which must be done if the Empire's to be saved.
Then Diocletian stirs himself and calls:
"Send me my secretary, there's work to do,
A despatch for the noble Caesar Maximian."

"To the Noble Caesar Maximian, etcetera, etcetera.
Greetings from Diocletian Augustus unto his son.

I have two despatches concerning Carausius' rising.
I need more facts before I can give advice.
I will list these below, but first remember clearly
All that you have achieved in less than a year,
The Bagaudae cleared from Gaul, the towns relieved,
The German nations pushed back beyond the Rhine.
Know Maximian that I have been impressed
By all that you have done and with the speed.
You are indeed a very Hercules.

Now to the questions and answers I need to know.
Which units have declared for Carausius?
Are they complete or detachments which he has?
Is it only Britain which Carausius holds
Or has he forces still in mainland Gaul?
I need to know the extent of the land he holds.
What title has he claimed? Has he issued coins?
What are the names and ranks of his support?
How substantial in fact is this devious revolt?
And what are your resources at this time?
How do you rate the loyalty of your troops?
What is the general state of the German tribes,
Do they remain quiet or do they seek to take
Advantage of this British rebellion?
That I think, my son, is quite enough,
But I hope these many questions emphasise
My very real concern for your well being.
I have great confidence in you, Maximian.
Impatiently I wait to hear your news.

From Diocletian Augustus, accept my good wishes. Farewell."

More waiting, and more time to contemplate,
While the other business of the court proceeds,
Time to worry that everything has been done,

THE EXERCISE OF AUTHORITY

Which could be done and at the proper time.
Not days but weeks must pass before he will hear
More definite news from Maximian in the west.

— ※ —

At last it came, the despatch with the order of battle
Of the self-styled Carausius Augustus, Restorer of Britain,
With Maximian's assessment of the threat this usurper posed.
Diocletian carefully considered this latest despatch.
He tried to guess what Aurelian would have done,
No need to guess! He would have gone to help,
No waiting about, he would have rushed to war.

But Maximian was *his* helpmeet, his Hercules,
He would not succeed, if in every crisis
Diocletian immediately came rushing to his support.
This crisis showed Maximian to be loyal,
Other lieutenants faced with usurpation,
With a rival Augustus claiming ultimate power,
Would not have waited, however good the advice
Which might come from the other end of the world.
They would have called themselves Augustus too.

Imperial stability required two Emperors.
Augustus and his Caesar was not enough.
Two separate but indivisible heads of state.
The Antonines had done this a hundred years ago,
But the second Augustus then had been a cypher,
But it was a precedent and the best ideas
Develop naturally from experience in the past.

— ※ —

"To the Noble Caesar Maximian, etcetera, etcetera.
Greetings from Diocletian Augustus unto his son.

For long I have thought about Carausius.
His position for the moment seems very strong indeed,
But he lacks one thing – legal authority.
We must do nothing which could legitimise
His arbitrary act of seizing power in Britain;
No treaties, talks informal or otherwise
Which could be construed by him to imply recognition.

DIOCLETIAN

You need time to build yourself another fleet
And time to isolate his allies, the Franks,
Who with the land at the mouth of the River Rhine
Are essential to him in holding the narrow sea.
But first you have to dominate those tribes
Joined together further up the Rhine.
It is there in the coming season you need to be.
Meanwhile ensure Carausius does not attack
By sending cunning agents and counter-spies,
Who will let Carausius think that he is safe
Providing he does not provoke you with rash acts.

Maximian, know that once I had a dream,
Shortly after assuming the imperial power,
In which Great Jove and the noble Hercules
Showed me clearly all that we have to do
That we may save the Empire and it will last
Safe and strong, another thousand years.
But first we need imperial stability
To be exercised with legitimate authority
In every province of the Empire, in every town.
You are my Hercules, my strong right arm
As close to me as Hercules to Jove.
As proof of this I am sending you this cloak,
Which long ago the great Aurelian wore
Of rare design of Indian sandyx made,
A garment which only Augustus himself can wear,
And wear it you will, for Maximian I need your help
As a brother in our imperial enterprise.
Will you join me as Augustus, with all powers
Appertaining to the office of Emperor,
Holding them jointly and indivisibly
With me, your brother, so we will rule the world?

I suggest you go to Milan without delay
And have yourself proclaimed Augustus there,
With ceremony emphasising legal right,
And take the family name of Hercules.
Meanwhile my family will be named for Jove,
And I will adopt your name of Aurelius,
To signify the closeness of the bond
Between us two as Brother Emperors.

THE EXERCISE OF AUTHORITY

I am constrained to stay here in the east,
The Persian frontier needs be organised,
The nations press against the Danube line.
By formal edict I will make it clear
That I adopt you Brother, Maximian,
Augustus, and partner, with all authority.

I also send you our friend Constantius Chlorus,
He is an able and experienced officer,
On whom you can rely in the coming wars
Both on the Rhine and against Carausius.

Go well, Brother, succeed in all you do,
For what you do yourself, you do for me.

From Diocletian Augustus unto his brother, Maximian,
Accept my sincere fraternal good wishes. Farewell."

The Emperor Comes APRIL 286
aet. 42

In two days time the Emperor's retinue
Will enter Tyre, city of Phoenicia.
Late in Spring, the sun warm on the back,
The wind is cool, blowing off the sea,
The hillside full of colour, the grass still green,
The court's relaxed as if on holiday.

With winter done, it is the Emperor's pleasure
To see and to be seen by the citizens,
So they may know they have an Emperor
Who is concerned with the ordinary peoples' lot.
He's passed through the coasts of Syria and now is set
For Tiberias on the lake in Palestine.

The Emperor Diocletian is concerned
To know the state of the frontier provinces,
For Persia, no longer divided, is strong again,
Recovered from Carus' sack of Ctesiphon,
And now presents a threat to all the East
Which the Emperor on his progress would assess.

It deep midwinter the original plans were made
To progress throughout the provinces of the East
When the days lengthened and the mountain passes cleared.

DIOCLETIAN

All then was activity and busy-ness,
Messages to and fro, that one Spring day
The Emperor and his entourage could be
Riding along the road that leads to Tyre.

The Adventus

From where we stand high up on the hill
The Emperor's progress looks magnificent;
The advance guard halting at the city line
Waits for the reception party due from Tyre.

The people stream from every side to see
The Emperor, his entourage and all his power,
The soldiers in their uniforms, the flags,
The Eagles with their escort, the proud men
Who ride beside the one who all would see,
The Emperor in person acknowledging the shouts
Of all the ordinary people who line the way.
More come running, the herdsmen leave their flocks,
Fishermen desert their nets, the fish are free.
Villagers report the scene, so even more
Crowd the way to greet their Imperial Lord.

Here comes the council president of Tyre,
Escorted by members of the city watch,
Smartly dressed in civic uniforms,
Specially designed in honour of this day.
They glow with pride as the council president
Performs the visit's opening ceremony.

Above the hubbub, we hear the president's voice
Demanding to know who travels on the road.
The imperial herald formally responds:
"Imperator Caesar, Lord of all the world,
Gaius Aurelius Valerius Diocletianus
Pius Felix Invictus Augustus requires
The right of way to enter his city of Tyre."

The president dismounts and humbly kneels,
Presents the city keys and begins to speak.
It is a speech which the Emperor's company

THE EXERCISE OF AUTHORITY

Have on this progress heard so many times,
Familiar indeed, but genuine nonetheless,
Expressing the peoples' loyalty and joy
That the divine Augustus condescends to walk
Among the Empire's humble citizens.

The Emperor briefly acknowledges the speech;
The keys of Tyre are graciously returned.
The president with the constables escort
The Emperor and his party through the fields
Between the crowds towards the city walls.

Thr procession halts before the city gates;
There the altar is lit, libations poured,
Sweet smell of incense, the blood of sacrifice
In particular honour of the god of the city gate.

The party proceeds, the excited spectators' shouts
Drown the strident music of the city band.
They pass through the narrow street, all decked with flowers,
The banners of the guilds, the freshly whitewashed walls,
Every street and pavement newly swept
Ready for this visit of the Emperor.

On the steps of the basileia, specially kept
As a house for kings since very ancient times,
The council waits to greet their Emperor.
The party enters the forum, there is a roar
From excited Tyreens, the breathless band plays on.
More speeches, libations poured and incense thrown,
A sacrifice of thanks to the god of Tyre
That the Emperor had safely come to be with them.

Briefing the Emperor

"Pray let me know the order of the day.
At what hour do they plan the market dedication?"
Diocletian as was his custom liked to review
The business that was to be done on the coming day.
They were in the basileia late at night,
The welcoming feast was done, their hosts had gone.

DIOCLETIAN

The Master of Office consulted his various lists:
"At the salutation in the morning there will be
The embassy from Cyrene who seek redress
Of impositions placed on them before…"

"Have they submitted a summary of their case?"

"Not yet, my Lord, that they will do tomorrow.
Besides there will be other petitioners,
Which we will have to limit to allow the time
For you to confer with the Governor and legionary Legates
On the province's defence from persistent desert raids.
The dedication of the new marketplace
Will start at the sixth hour and probably last till the eighth.
We then progress to the theatre, to review
The procession of the city guilds and businesses
Which flourish here providing the wealth of Tyre."

"Do they understand the choice of Hercules
To be the tutelary god of their marketplace?"

"I doubt it, my lord, there're jokes about a broom
Being the secret weapon of Hercules."

"I must emphasise the link with my Brother's house
And explain the relation of Hercules to Jove.
Is my secretary there so I can check my speech?
Has the amount of dues to be cancelled been agreed?
It must be enough to be significant,
But not so much that the treasury feels the pinch."

The Praetorian Prefect came forward to answer him,
(It was Hannibalianus who had assumed the post
When the armies of Carus had finally been absorbed):
"Five years imperial share of the market dues
Has been proposed but confirmation is needed
That the Master of Sacrae Largitiones agrees."

"Agree together before the Salutations
That I may then consider and decide,
So we can indicate to the men of Tyre
Our pleasure in this matter when we meet
To dedicate their market to Hercules."

THE EXERCISE OF AUTHORITY

And then the Emperor rose and turned to bed,
His counsellors and companions withdrew.
His chamberlains and body servant stayed
Until he finally was prepared for sleep.
So much to do, so little time to ensure
The very survival of the Roman world.

Work in Progress

Two days on, the Emperor is south of Tyre
Acknowledging the shouts of greeting from the crowd
Riding at ease in the midst of his company
With the Praetorian Prefect immediately by his side,
And on the other whomever he might wish to call;
For time is scarce, the business must be done
Even on progress on the imperial way.

The Emperor has called his legal secretary
To report the present status of requests
For legal rulings which he has in hand.

"Tell me, Gregorius, how many requests you have.
We received a number while we were in Tyre.
What do you make of the petition we've had from Cyrene?
I don't want to keep them trailing along with us."

"My lord, I've prepared a number for you to review.
The case of Cyrene is disputed, a hearing is required.
Shall I arrange for this in Tiberias when we will have time?"

This was agreed and then the Emperor questioned
How Gregorius recorded the many legal decisions,
How many clerks and assistants he had travelling with him,
How the records were carried and later how they were published,
And then the Emperor instructed his secretary Gregorius:

"I am determined that the due process of law
Shall function once again now there is peace.
Pure legal principles must be preserved.
We must ensure our rulings reaffirm
The basic essentials of good Roman law

DIOCLETIAN

Avoiding any distortions and influences
Which may emanate from the Orient or from Greece.
I want you to keep a careful register
Of all the legal decisions which we give,
With a summary of all enactments and rulings made
Since the time that the divine Hadrian was with us,
And have these distributed to every province.

Furthermore it is essential that the governor
In each and every province makes the law
Readily available to all who seek redress.
Draft for me instructions to this effect.

How do you assess the visit, Praetorian Prefect?
The people of Tyre seemed pleased to have us among them."

"They were certainly pleased, my lord. The visit went well.
The remission of dues, I think, was well received.
That probably balanced the additional cost of our stay."
Hannibalianus laughed as he said these words,
But the Emperor considered the matter more seriously.

"I am very concerned how many decurions,
On whom the administration of our cities depend,
Appear less and less inclined to fulfil their duties.
Some exchange their land so they are disqualified,
Others join the army, or just withdraw themselves
To their estates many miles away.
They consider the burden of service to the city
Outweighs the honour. They completely ignore their duty.
The decurion class is essential in the imperial structure.

Secretary Gregorius, please prepare me a draft
Of regulations, that we may consider together,
Which will ensure that decurions stay in their cities
Until they have finished their various levels of service."

And then the Emperor turned to greet the crowds
More came from every side, across the fields,
Nothing would stand in their way; they would see their lord
But little thought that amongst this show and pomp,
They were witnessing the Emperor at work.

THE EXERCISE OF AUTHORITY

Persicus Maximus

EMESA
AD 287
aet. 43

"May I introduce myself? I am Bagavan,
A humble servant of the King of Kings.
I am deputy chamberlain at my master's court
Temporarily seconded to lead this embassy.
My family has served the royal Sassanid house
From the very day that Ardashir was crowned,
Once more establishing the ancient faith
Of Zoroaster, purified in fire,
When the Persian Empire became a power again.

My family evidently has the skill
In matters diplomatic, for we are called
Whenever foreign powers would be addressed.
We seem to have an instinct for the art
Of conveying thoughts from one proud man to another;
How to be fierce without hurting pride,
How to be friendly without appearing weak,
Clearly distinguishing the messenger from the message,
How to listen and how to identify
The difference between what is said and what is thought;
How to observe all those tell-tale signs
Which indicate the health of a foreign power,
For nations, just as men, flourish and fail,
And knowing the signs is the essence of diplomacy.

Here we are for instance in the city of Emesa;
It is not by chance that it is here we meet,
For outside this town the great Aurelian
Defeated the Queen Zenobia, and on that day
The servants of the Sun God were seen in the Roman ranks,
Shoulder to shoulder, they brought them victory.
The message these Romans would give is clear enough.

I assisted once on a previous embassy
But the two could hardly be more different.
My uncle led that mission. I recall it well:
The Roman army encamped high on a hill
Above the Euphrates, a windy day in Spring,
We approached their camp at dusk, the fires were lit
Round one a group of officers, who turned to us

DIOCLETIAN

As if we were travellers looking for a bed,
Not representatives of the King of Kings.
My uncle did his best to present our case
But the old man, their leader, sitting there just stared,
(I remember the shock on seeing his purple cloak)
When my uncle finished the old man turned and faced us,
He removed his cap, it was cold on the mountain top,
And then he said, pointing to his pate:
'I will leave the plain of Persia just like this,
Not a single tree, not even a blade of grass.'
I remember shivering as I looked at the bald old man.

It may make a good tale but not good diplomacy.
Carus, for it was the Emperor Carus that night
Who threatened us on the top of the windy hill,
So impressed us that we reported to our king
That the Roman power would not negotiate
So our king withdrew – he had troubles enough elsewhere,
And the Romans were drawn into the empty land,
No foe to fight, no aim, no war to win.

What a contrast here in this new Emperor.
Here there's a feeling of stability over all
Which has its source in the Emperor's very being;
It is not only what he says but how he says it.

First, the formality which is familiar
To one who comes from the court of the King of Kings.
We see the Augustus only with ceremony;
Properly received into the presence, we wait,
The veil is removed, the Emperor revealed on high,
Seated in pomp, radiate crowned and garbed.

Second, the evidence of the army ready for war,
The legions at his call, fully equipped and trained,
The cavalry, beautifully turned out, eager to fight,
All there plain to see, not commented on.
The forts rebuilt, stronger than ever before,
Storehouses and granaries with new defensive walls,
Villages now are strongpoints, defence in depth,
Present much greater obstacles, if we attacked.
Circesium on the frontier, with its new walls,
We saw ourselves as we set out on this mission.

THE EXERCISE OF AUTHORITY

Third, the Roman message is simple and clear,
Not a generalised threat of destroying trees and grass,
But recognition of their rule in Mesopotamia
And their right to confirm the king of Armenia.
With this agreed all will be friendship and light
Between the greatest Empires of the World.

I cannot say I like it and I have said as much
In the despatches I have sent to Vahram, our king.
The key to the control of the frontier has always been
Armenia, in the mountain fastness, to the north.
The great Sapor gained the right to name
The client king, when Valerian was overthrown.
But my king is tired, with many a threat elsewhere.
He asks me if we can trust this new man's word;
I have to say we can, of that I am sure,
So tomorrow I must present my king's reply.
We will accept their demands and trust their word,
And hope to live in peace and amity,
Until another king, another chance,
To test again the strength of the Roman power."

— * —

So Diocletian won his greatest victory
Against a foreign power, without a blow,
No blood was spilt, no countryside laid waste.
The Persian frontier remained at peace for years,
Long enough to establish his military power
Along the Danube and in Raetia,
In support of his brother Maximian, who in the west
Campaigned against the nations across the Rhine.
Together they fixed the northern frontier line
With fortresses reinforced and deep defence.
Many new legions, cavalry and frontier troops
Were raised to man the forts and hold the line
So the Barbarian tribes were unable to break through,
And the citizens of the Empire could live in peace.

SO MUCH TO DO
in which the many problems facing the Empire require of Diocletian new solutions

God Sees All

Jupiter watched, pleased with what he saw.
It seemed his devotee would stem the tide
Of northern nations pressing against the line,
And establish peace in the Empire far and wide.

That he must succeed was essential to the god,
For the omniscient Jove was only too aware
That gods remain in heaven only so long
As they are of use to men, who put them there.

Throughout the East new mysteries abound,
Which year by year suborn the peoples' hearts
With promises of life when this one is done,
That after present anguish perfection starts.

Jupiter admired the wisdom of this man,
That he had shared his power and shared the task
With his brother Emperor, for the task was more
Than one could undertake or the gods should ask.

But if it proved too much for these two men,
If the Empire was destroyed in spite of Jove,
Then another god and religion from the East,
Might win despite how hard these two men strove.

DIOCLETIAN

What if the deepest thoughts of this devotee
Should conclude at length the Empire would not survive
Without support of the new god from the East –
How then would the Olympian gods remain alive?

Already the man had shared his power and task;
Could he be encouraged to share his power again?
And if with one who respected the ancient gods,
Then Jupiter might his omnipotence retain.

Jupiter considered with care all those at court,
Looked into the deepest crannies of each man's mind
Seeking one, in whom authority to rule
And loyalty to the ancient gods, combined.

And such a one was the young Galerius,
Raised as a shepherd in the wild countryside,
A man who had witnessed nature's basic power
And in the ancient Roman verities took pride.

Close Call

PANNONIA
AD 288
aet. 44

"That was close. Far too close for comfort.
I am an old fox and should have behaved as such.
But for the prompt intervention of the young tribune
I would have become a name in a history book.

Now that I am back in my quarters and have had a bath,
I can recall the incident in full.
What a fool I was! I am meant to be Emperor –
And if the Sarmatian horsemen had found their mark,
They would have fixed Diocletian, the Empire – all.

I was so certain all those years ago
That Aurelian was foolish to put the world at risk
In every battle, skirmish and foray.
I considered him foolhardy in doing that,
And here I am doing precisely the same.

In the last few years we have strengthened our defences
As the river flows south in Lower Pannonia.
We have established a number of fortified landing points
Opposite the major forts which we have rebuilt.

SO MUCH TO DO

From these points across the river we can observe
The movements of the Sarmatians and be prepared –
But evidently not enough! – I'd expressed a wish
To see the defensive system and how it worked.
Frankly I was bored with the affairs of state
And wanted to walk around and see for myself –
The thunder in the air was unsettling everyone.

It was agreed, in order to avoid too much attention,
I would go incognito – just a small escort.
But the young tribune at the crossing saw me pass,
He must have recognised me, and as things turned out
This was just as well – still I shudder to think!
We were proceeding towards one of the lookout posts
The track passed by a thicket and some reeds,
When suddenly a shout, and there the Sarmatian horse
Came charging down the road, caught us off guard –
More shouts behind, another Sarmatian group
Came at us out of the reedbeds – we were cut off.

I remember thinking this is hardly the way to act
The part of the Emperor of the Roman World.
The sky darkened, the heat closed in on us,
I sat my horse, my escort surrounding me,
We watched the Sarmatian warriors circling round.
It grew darker yet, the roaring of the wind,
We could hardly see the Sarmatians or they see us.

And suddenly we were saved – the lightning struck,
Lightning such as I had never seen before.
The whole sky lit up, all was white and clear,
Behold devastation in the Sarmatian ranks.
The thunderbolt had struck the leading group;
By successive lightning flashes, we could see
Reinforcements riding pellmell up the road,
The young tribune charging ahead, streaming with rain.
The Sarmatians scattered as quickly as they had appeared
And we withdrew as the thunder rolled away."

It was many hours later that night that the Emperor conferred
How best to handle the incident which had occurred.
But what had occurred? Had the Emperor been attacked?

DIOCLETIAN

Not necessarily so – he had been incognito.
But surely the Sarmatians had attacked close to the line,
For this the Roman Power must remonstrate.
But the local chief had immediately indicated
That the attack had been performed by renegades.
Those of them that had survived the lightning strike
Had not survived the anger of their chief.
Furthermore the Sarmatians showed no sign they knew
How close they had been to the end of an imperial reign.
As policy required that peace should yet prevail
That the defences along the river could be improved,
As soon as the counsellors understood the drift
Of their master's mind that evening after the storm,
It was agreed to accept the Sarmatian plea
That renegades had failed to keep the peace,
Subject to payment of certain fines and promises
Of service of Sarmatian cavalry in the Orient.

As they prepare to leave, the Emperor Diocletian spoke:
"I would have the tribune who was of service today
Brought here to court so I may speak with him.
We are indebted to him, and to Jupiter.
I saw today the God's mysterious ways."

And so it was that Galerius came to court.

Brothers' Meeting

AD 288
aet. 44

It was late in the season when the brother Emperors met
In the city of Mainz, headquarters of Maximian,
No great ceremony, much more a council of war,
To review their progress in making the Empire safe.

"Well met, Brother. I'm glad to hold your hand.
It is one thing to read your letters…"

                    "But not as good
As seeing face to face and hearing words."

"For me the one regret I have…"

                    "Me too!
I don't like not seeing you. I like the job!

SO MUCH TO DO

But if we could meet more often, it would be ideal."

"Maximian, you have not changed. You still rush in
And finish my thoughts before I've had the chance
Of fully developing what I wish to say.
But it's good to see you, Brother, that's for sure.
In these few days we must work out detailed plans
How we can make the most of the advantages
You've gained here on the Rhine…"

"And we'll find time
To feast and celebrate our victories,
For I'm only too aware that it is one for all,
And all for one. The victories which I've gained
Would not have been, without your advice and help."

"Generous, my friend. By the gods, I'm glad we're here.
Let us show our heartfelt thanks with sacrifice.
And then we must plan, Maximian, there's much to do."

The Conference at Mainz   AD 288
aet. 44

"I, Afranius Hannibalianus
Was present at that conference at Mainz.
I little thought that, at that time, I saw
The four men in one room who would rule the world.

Diocletian had already achieved his power.
Of no great stature but still he looked the part,
There was about him a sense of authority,
A feeling of great confidence and strength,
He dominated any meeting by being there.
I was his Praetorian Prefect at the time,
Had served with him for years and seen him grow
From being a careful colleague, who thought a lot,
Into a ruler who understood the way
The complex system of the Empire worked,
On whose judgement all of us relied.
Indeed he was a man necessary for the state.

Maximian, of course, I knew in a different way.
He had married my daughter many years ago,

DIOCLETIAN

Briefly, for they had a child and my daughter died,
The child Theodora lived, she is here in Mainz.
Maximian is a bull of a man and acts like one,
His physical power fills the space around him,
Fierce in anger, fierce in friendship too.
Nothing, but nothing, will stand in his impetuous way,
Except the considered advice of Diocletian,
A very Hercules to Jupiter,
A strong right arm for the cunning careful brain.

Constantius was Maximian's Praetorian Prefect.
Being my opposite number at the conference,
I got to know him well, and liked him too.
He had been a protector as we all had been
And served in Syria under Aurelian;
He was of good birth, unlike many of us!
A moderate man, but a fighter nonetheless,
He made an effective contrast to his chief,
So when promoted Caesar in due course,
It seemed natural; that came as no surprise –
But the surprise for me was when my Theodora,
Maximian's daughter was offered him as wife,
Thus enrolling him in the family of Hercules.

Galerius, at that time, none of us knew well.
I remember being asked who the young man was.
He looked like a younger Maximian, fresh and keen,
They said he had been a shepherd before he joined.
He had come to Diocletian's notice on the last campaign,
He had been involved with distinction in a minor engagement,
And now was attached to the Emperor's personal staff.
If I had known that he would follow me
As Praetorian Prefect to the Emperor Diocletian,
And then be named Caesar of the Jovian house,
I would have paid the young man more attention,
As one deserves who is destined to reach the heights.

The conference itself concerned the northern line
And how we could work together to better effect.

SO MUCH TO DO

We planned a joint attack on the Alemanni,
Whose people had settled themselves among the hills,
Between the source of the Danube and the Rhine.
This was executed in the following year.
We also talked about the British problem,
Carausius still controlled the narrow sea.
Maximian was confident he would have sufficient ships
To retake the province before the year was out;
In spite of all our hopes this was not to be.

Above all I remember the conference as one of good will.
Here were two brothers planning how best to preserve
All that was good in the Empire to which they were called.
Not scheming against each other, but working together,
Proving thereby the genius of the one Diocletian,
The only one able to lead us out of our troubles."

— * —

A thousand miles from Mainz to Sirmium,
A city full of family memories,
It was there that the Emperor wished to celebrate
The ancient feast of the Saturnalia.
The conference with Maximian dragged on and on,
The officers on the Emperor's staff despaired
That the plans for the journey home they had carefully made
Would ever be fulfilled in actual fact.

At last the final banquet and sacrifice,
The brothers swore their mutual devotion and trust,
Embraced each other as military men will do,
And then Diocletian, his escort and entourage,
Were on their way posting up the Rhine,
With couriers racing ahead to alert each town
That the Emperor was at last about to come.

In spite of all their planning and despatch,
The autumn gales had stripped the tall trees bare,
Dank leaves below, the glorious colour gone,
Winter wet and cold was everywhere,
Before they reached the city of Sirmium.

DIOCLETIAN

Saturnalia

Since earliest times when men first saw the sun
And observed the length of day grow less and less,
They thought, with fear, they saw the sun's slow death
Until that shortest day when wasting ceased.

Regularly men have marked the reprieve thus won,
New life again which all can now possess,
And everyone can take another breath,
Live once again, the greatest and the least.

In joyful harmony, let every man and child rejoice,
At Saturnalia, New Year, Christmas – take your choice.

Anticipation

NICOMEDIA
AD 288
aet. 45

"Tell me Nurse, all about Sirmium.
Isn't it exciting my Father's sent for us?
We're going to join him for the Saturnalia.
I haven't seen him for many many years,
I cannot count how many, it's been so long.
Do you think he'll approve of me and how I've grown?
I was just a little girl when last we met,
And now…"

"…And now you're a lady. You must act the part
As a lady should. No hoydenish japes, young Miss.
At court demure deportment at all times
For you're the only daughter of the Emperor,
And don't forget it…"

"…But Nurse, it will be fun?
Here in Nicomedia, what's there to see?
Who is there to talk to? Only my Tutor and you."

"Only, indeed! There's gratitude for you!
I've half a mind to forget about Sirmium,
The lovely things that happened when I was young."

"Oh please, dear Nurse, of course I'm never bored,
Or hardly ever, not when you tell me tales,
Tales of when you were young in Sirmium,
And when my mother was a little girl

SO MUCH TO DO

About my age, all of eleven years.
That's not really little, it is old enough
To know one's not grown up, but almost so.
And can I take my kitten? And what about lessons?
Will I have to do them as we journey to Sirmium?"

"Keep still, Valeria, do not jump about.
You ask so many questions, but look who comes!
Your Mother looks pleased to me with this latest news.
Madam…"

    "Greetings, Good Nurse. We leave tomorrow,
Is all prepared?"

    "Tomorrow? Is all prepared!
Indeed it's not. Typical. No warning word,
Just a nod, and off we go, and nothing washed!
Excuse me, Madam, while I see to things.
The Lady Valeria indeed must look the part."

"Good morning, Child. I trust that you are prepared
For this sudden change, for this journey to the court.
Nurse will see that you have all you need,
In spite of all her grumbling, you will be dressed
As well as any lady at the court.
But Valeria, my dear, are you prepared yourself?"

"What do you mean, Mama – Am I prepared myself?
I'm going to see my father, isn't that enough?"

"Your father is the Emperor, and that above all else.
Everyone all the time depends on him,
Demands his time."

    "Is that the reason why
We never see him, he's always somewhere else?"

"Valeria, Child, there you go again!
You really must observe the golden rule:
Listen to people and let them finish their thought
Before you rush in with questions or observations.
You really must and particularly at the court."

"But Mother, people take so long to speak.
I can see the end of their thought before they do,

DIOCLETIAN

And I often forget my own if I have to wait!"

"My dear…"

"My Father. Tell me, what is he like?
It is so long since I saw him. I was a child."

"What is he like? How do you describe
Your right arm, your foot, your thigh, your skin –
It is part of you, yet also separate.
So it is with the man you are born to love,
If the gods are kind and bless you in that way.
And even if you are kept apart like us,
Your man remains as close as thigh or skin."

"Mother, you glow when you speak of my father so –
But what's he like? Will he approve of me?"

"Approve of you? Oh Yes! Of course, my dear.
You have grown into a lady. You must act the part.
No sudden fits of giggles, no silly games.
Keep still, straight back, hands crossed, avert your eyes.
You know the rules."

"But when it itches, what then?
But tell me of my father."

"He is a man,
And being a man he is busy all the time
With facts, with things, with the affairs of state.
He has asked for us to join him for Saturnalia,
But he will be occupied for much of the time.
Remember that does not mean he doesn't love you,
But that he is the man on whom the Empire rests.
Every action, every decision that is made
Begins with him and the results return to him.
He has an ability to see how things connect
More thoroughly than is seen by other men,
And that is why men listen with respect
When my lord, your father, Diocletian speaks."

"What a man my father is! But he will have time
To talk to me, for it is the Saturnalia.
Then all things are changed. Everything's upside down.
The slaves are masters; we act the servants' part.

SO MUCH TO DO

The Emperor has to wear the freedman's cap."

"I doubt if your father will observe that part of the custom.
It is not in his nature to easily play the fool."

"But he must relax and when he does, you'll see,
He will notice me and we will talk and talk.
I am so happy. I am going to see my father,
He will notice me and we will talk and talk."

A Domestic Scene

SIRMIUM
AD 288
aet. 45

In the event both mother and daughter were right.
Her husband *was* concerned with the affairs of state,
His busy mind was full of work in progress.
He felt uneasy with the Saturnalia,
With its topsy-turvy customs and all the fun.
He was safer with the formality of the court,
Where everyone knew their place and played their part.

But he was a man who observed the ancient rites;
He was present when his staff served the servants' meal;
For the briefest moment he wore the freedman's cap;
He drew the lots for presents for all the staff;
And drew a sigh of relief when he could withdraw
To dine with his close family according to custom,
And after that he sat with his womenfolk,
And so his daughter was proved right – they talked.

[She has grown. Almost a young lady. I like her style –
Her determination, her high seriousness.
Her fine looks, it is amazing how young women
Learn to look the part. Now what is that she says?]

[I don't think he's listening, there's mist behind his eyes
How can I get him to concentrate on me?
Dear gods inspire me, make me interesting.
Do you think he would appreciate my kittens' games?]

[She is almost old enough to attract the men.
Today I saw how often she caught their eye.
They were surprised, I guess, that this old block
Had produced so promising a sapling here.]

DIOCLETIAN

[Oh what can I say. He almost smiles, and yet
There's mist behind those eyes. He is far away.
What can I do to bring him back to me?
What is he thinking of? I wish I knew.]

[A few more years, and she'll be her mother's age
When I came to Sirmium all those years ago.
There Prisca quietly sits watching us both
With fondness as our daughter entertains
This dry old man with serious conversation.]

"...And so my kitten is now the wisest cat,
Though I don't think my tutor appreciates the fact."
[I don't think he heard a word of all I said.
What a waste for the tale of the cat was really funny.
I will just sit quietly and wait till he speaks to me.]

[Soon we will have to find a man for her.
She will be a gift for a strong determined man
And a gift to me for she will bring me a son.
It's becoming clear that Maximian and I alone
Cannot maintain the peace and hold the line.
Somehow we have to extend the imperial power,
With further legions and many more frontier troops.
How can we pay for all these new recruits?
We've expanded the army but the cost is not evenly borne.
We need to establish that everyone must pay,
Not just those provinces close to the battle zone.
Now how can we do that? – What is that she says?
This is a family feast – I must concentrate.]

"Sir, I did not speak. I waited for you."

"Tell me, Valeria, what of your studies then.
Your tutor reports that you are diligent,
Though concerned perhaps too much with animals,
Particularly those of the cuddly furry kind..."

And as she talked her father's busy mind
Visited all the current work in progress:
How the taxation system could be further developed
So that it was fairer and more general;

THE EXERCISE OF AUTHORITY

The new building works in Nicomedia
And here in Sirmium were well in hand,
So necessary as a setting for the Emperor's power,
But craftsmen were required, they must be paid,
For the imperial treasury yet another call.

But when the day was done he felt relaxed;
His bright young daughter proved a refreshing change
From the careful courtiers and the military men.
It was no surprise to Prisca, who had watched it all,
When the Emperor requested they both delay their return
As he could see more of his daughter in Sirmium.

But even Prisca didn't follow his deeper thoughts,
How he needed more men to carry the imperial load,
Men who were young, who would share in the Empire's defence,
Sons in the families of Jove and of Hercules,
And how Valeria would help him find such a son.

THE NEED TO SHARE THE LOAD
in which Diocletian plans and with patience prepares his colleagues for new solutions

The Panegyrist's Complaint EARLY 291
aet. 47

"The composition of an imperial panegyric
Does not come to one easily; it is an art,
And like so many arts, depends on sweat.
There is a traditional structure which must be observed –
First the subject is compared to former rulers,
Then to the heroes of the past, and then to the gods,
All to their disfavour whoever you choose,
For at the moment of the oration there is only one,
Only one object of the world's regard and praise.
All this must be expressed with eloquence
Of such perfection that every heart is turned,
The natural course of everyone is stopped,
Overcome by the innate beauty, strong men weep,
And lesser men feel greater for the hearing of it.

Flattery dulls the judgement of most men,
Which is fortunate for the striving panegyrist
For otherwise the work would be impossible!

And now I, Mamertinus, have a fearful task,
For the Brother Augusti have chosen to celebrate
The opening of the fifth year of their fraternal reign
By meeting together in the City of Milan,
And as I am well known for my panegyrics
My master Maximian has commanded that I have one prepared.

DIOCLETIAN

A panegyric for the two most powerful men –
I am weak with fear – the thought of facing them,
Speaking my thoughts with no one in between
To shield me from the penetrating gaze
Of the two men who dominate our world.
A single subject can prove hard enough,
But a double one may prove the end of me.

How to praise the one without offending the other?
But I have been instructed to emphasise
The fraternal unity of these all powerful men
So I will carefully navigate a course
Between my man's fierceness and the other's pride.
Indeed I will emphasis their unity
By balancing each of their triumphs and victories.

A balancing act which will prove difficult
As these two men work in such different ways.
Maximian loves a battle, is restless at peace;
His victories, he earned himself with his own hand.
But the Senior Augustus is made of more complex stuff,
He uses others to fight whenever he can
But is there to plan the strategy and make the peace.
He is fortunate in having many able men
Who are loyal to him, prepared to fight his wars.
He has as Praetorian Prefect, Hannibalianus,
Who is indeed experienced and now I hear
He has a new man, Galerius, who is just as good.
But when I balance the treaties which they have made
I must admit the one with the Persian power
Which Diocletian's made, far outstrips
Anything which Maximian has achieved.

The meeting will be in Milan and not in Rome,
Which I understand is a question of policy.
The Senate will have to send a delegation
And this is a point I am told I must emphasise.
My panegyric should be a piece of art
Whereas in fact it is pure politics.

I must to work, this is the time for sweat.
Having had the draft approved by Constantius
(He is my mentor for he brought me to the court)

THE NEED TO SHARE THE LOAD

I plan to delay the final composition
Until the very eve for then I can
Describe the excitement of the happy day
When the Masters of the World rejoice together."

Preparing for the Meeting   AD 291
aet. 47

The meeting in Milan had need of thorough planning
If it was to succeed in showing everyone
That Diocletian and Maximian
Together in felicity ruled the world.
Each imperial progress had to be carefully planned
As it converged on the city of Milan
That time be allowed for the Emperor at every town
To be received with honour and be seen
But still arrive at the same hour in the end.
The formal meeting itself must be agreed,
The ceremonial, the panegyric, the pomp,
All needed checking and agreeing between the courts.

For the Emperor Diocletian there were two men
Who had the duty of ensuring all went well.
The Master of Office and Praetorian Prefect
Met yet again to check all had been done.

"Well, Prefect, there's a limit to what mere men can do.
However much we plan, the gods decide.
Let us hope their plans agree with those we've made!
But apart from the questions of ceremonial,
We have to prepare the list for the Emperor
Of the various matters requiring resolution
For the better development of the Empire's governance."

Item. Defence of the realm. Northern Tier.
Item. Status of Britain. Recovery plan.
Item. Relations with Persia. Current update.
Item. Egypt. The Blemmyes attack on trade.
Item. Defence of the realm. Southern Tier.

Item. Increasing the legions and frontier troops.

Item. Taxation. Agreement on general capitation.
Item. Currency reform. Progress report.

DIOCLETIAN

— ✳ —

The Emperor was alone when he reviewed the list.
He knew that all the items must be discussed,
But did the people understand how every item connected;
Did they sense over all the power of mighty Jove?
For five long years they had held the northern line
And gradually had the defences reinforced.
If the Persians broke the treaty before all this was done
Or if war broke out in Egypt or Africa,
Had they enough resources to keep the peace?

All the while Britain and the coasts of Gaul
Were in the hands of that Carausius,
Whose very existence remained a running sore.

A further increase in the military establishment
Was surely required to meet these many demands.
All this must be paid for, everyone must be assessed,
Not just the provinces close to the frontier line,
No arbitrary seizure but strictly according to the law,
Payment in kind but also in currency
But this needs reforming and silver's in short supply.
The only sound coin comes from Carausius –
Always Carausius. He must be brought to heel!

So much to do, almost more to bear
Than two can do, however dedicated.
A private item to be discussed at length
Must be the need of help for both of us.

But Maximian has his son, Maxentius,
And thinks of him as a Caesar in the making,
But he is too young. He needs one fully grown
To carry his share of the heavy imperial task,
Such a one as Constantius; he would fit the part,
But how to wean my friend from Maxentius?
If he adopted Constantius as his son
And gave him Theodora as his wife –
Maximian dotes on her and so this giving
Would act as a bonding of father and of son –
Then he would have a Caesar worth the name
And she could bear grandsons for Maximian.

THE NEED TO SHARE THE LOAD

But Constantius already has a full grown son –
People – but for people – plans could be easily made –
What is his name? – I think it is Constantine.
I will take the young man with me back to the East
And watch how he develops. We need good men.
And who should be my Caesar? I need a son.
Hannibalianus is certainly now too old.
Of the younger men Galerius springs to mind,
The eager young tribune Galerius of the rainswept hair.
But could he stand the bad years with the good?
I must see by giving him some larger tasks
And if he succeeds then he may be the man.

So here is this list of items to be discussed
When we meet together to celebrate in Milan.
But none as important as that close within my mind.
I will present them as the time and occasion allows,
So that the reign of Jove and Hercules
May last, and peace and felicity prevail.

And may they prevail and the people understand –
People – but for people – plans could be easily made.

— ∗ —

Since the meeting in Milan another year has passed, AD 292
Another year of defending the northern front, *aet.* 48
Extending walls, rebuilding fortresses.
Another year of watching the Persian realm
Where Vahram grows old, his vassals murmuring
Against the treaty he had made with Rome.
New legions raised for Jove and Hercules
With the Tribune Galerius commanding the Jovians.

The other items on the list will need much more time:
The careful plans for the currency reform
Require that silver should be in good supply,
Reducing Carausius entails another army,
And above all else Maximian needs the time
To accept the fact that he needs a Caesar now,
A strong right arm to fight for him in Gaul.

DIOCLETIAN

Certainty   Early 292
aet. 48

"Nurse, I've seen my man. He is for me."

"How can you possibly say that, Valeria?
You hardly know the man, or what he's like."

"How d'you know who I'm speaking of?"

                                 "I know!
I saw your eyes tethered to his face.
Whenever he spoke you watched with bated breath,
No demurely casting down your eyes.
With joy, you openly followed his every move."

"As soon as I saw him I knew…"

                         "Which is just as well,
For your father, they say, favours this young man,"

"Dear Nurse, talk to me of Gaius Galerius.
Tell me all you know about this man.
I can never tire of hearing talk of him.
What did you make of the interesting way he stood
And did you hear him laugh, a generous laugh,
And the broadness of his shoulders, his fine head.
Did you see him, Nurse. I know that he's my man."

Gossip   Early 292
aet. 48

"Have you heard the news?"

                         "Till you tell me, I cannot say."

"That Galerius has been named Praetorian Prefect!"

"What? Gaius Galerius, Legate of the Jovians?"

"The same…"

                 "But he has hardly been a year
Commanding the Jovians. Has he proved himself?"

"What need to prove yourself if the soft eyes
Of the Emperor's daughter kindly look on you?"

"But you do him wrong, he's a fine soldier too…

THE NEED TO SHARE THE LOAD

[We must watch our tongues. He's now a man of power.]
Not only commanding the Jovians but before
He showed a flair for leading men in war,
And he has another important attribute,
The flair for being just where the action is.
There is a rumour too that as a younger man
He saved the Emperor on the Sarmatian front.
The details are obscure, but it does prove my point
He has a knack of being there when needed.
But what of Afranius Hannibalianus,
Surely he's done a good job as Praetorian Prefect?"

"You know he has already been named ordinary consul
So the coming year will then be named for him.
The Emperor is therefore making it crystal clear
That he still holds Hannibalianus in high regard –
He must be the last of that small inner group
Who supported the Emperor when he came to power.
They all now have gone, with Maximian to the west,
The others scattered round the Empire, away from court –
Anyhow he is not as young as once he was,
Though no doubt the Emperor can think for all of us
He needs younger men to wield the fighting sword."

The Tower at Night

NICOMEDIA
EARLY 292
aet. 48

From where we stand at the corner of the square
We can see the light in the window of the tower.
It is always there late into the night
When other folk have long since gone to bed.
Only the sounds of the night watch remain
And the city of Nicomedia lies asleep.

The Emperor's palace, refurbished and rebuilt,
Dominates the square on the southern side.
Throughout the city new buildings accumulate,
For there is wealth wherever the Emperor is.
On the northern side of the square, a fine new church
Casts its shadow across the window of the tower.

DIOCLETIAN

Within the tower Diocletian contemplates
After the formal business of the day.
After the dinner and discussion with his guests
It is the Emperor's habit to withdraw
To his private room within the tower – and think,
For there alone he has the time to plan.

He is nearly ready to expand the imperial power,
Galerius has proved effective on the northern front,
There is news from Maximian he accepts Constantius,
Sons for the Houses of Jove and Hercules.
But with that, the provincial governments must be reviewed,
Reduced in size and power so they pose no threat.

The reorganisation of the revenue proceeds apace,
The plans are ready for the currency reform,
The army is expanded, the fortresses rebuilt,
The fragile frontiers hold and there is peace –
As long as the people acknowledge the ancient gods –
Thus late in the night in the tower, the Emperor thought.

Dear Confident One

Dear confident Valeria,
Bright of face, eager, keen,
Long may your certainty remain
That all things be as they have been.

The world has smiled on your young years,
You have responded, full of joy,
So everyone for you in turn
Gladly all their skills employ.

May this support and warmth bring strength
To help you in the years ahead
To persevere in this frightening world,
Fraught with disabling fears and dread.

In spite of whatever may befall
May your certainty remain,
And we be stronger for seeing you
Your calm confidence retain.

THE NEED TO SHARE THE LOAD

Need AD 292

"Has he come?"

        "Patience, Valeria, he'll come in time."
[In time, indeed, but will he be in time?]

"Did the messenger go last night? Nurse, will he come?"

"He went two days ago. He will come, my dear.
He will come as soon as he can get away –
The business of the frontier takes all his time –
Your father depends on him in so many ways."

"I know but I want him here. I think it's time."

"Rest easy, my pet, you must not fret yourself.
It does the babe no good, you fretting so.
Lie still. All is prepared. The midwife's here.
Have confidence, my dear, all will be well."

"But when will Galerius come? I need my lord."

"Soon, my pet, soon." [God knows how soon.
She worries far too much that he is not here,
How will she fare, and the babe yet to be born,
For I doubt if her busy lord will come in time,
She has need, for sure, of all our support and help
For I feel it is going to be a hard hard time
Bringing this one into this wicked world.]

Action at Last MARCH 293
aet. 49

Contemplation done, at last the time to act;
In the tenth year since the fatal boar was slain,
Diocletian after years of planning, moves.
And moves to such effect that all recall
The year imperial power was split in four.

The Brother Emperors each adopt a son:
Maximian takes Constantius unto his own,
Proclaims him Caesar in the family of Hercules.
Diocletian in Sirmium adopts Galerius,
A son to the family of Jupiter and Caesar in the East.
So the Emperor Diocletian formed the Tetrarchy,

DIOCLETIAN

The imperial power indivisible, wielded by four,
Guided with the authority of the one essential to the state.

Then all is action, pent-up plans unfurl,
Constantius proceeds against Carausius,
Clears the coasts of Gaul, invests Boulogne.
He builds a mole to block the harbour mouth
And cuts it off from help across the sea,
Boulogne then falls, and with it the Saxon Shore
No longer impregnable and Britain lies exposed.

Meanwhile the Caesar Galerius is despatched
To establish again in Egypt imperial power.
Long had the Blemmyes from Ethiopia
Interrupted trade from the Red Sea to the Nile.
This interruption Galerius peremptorily stopped.

At last the grey men of the treasury confirmed
That all was ready for the currency reform.
With bullion sufficient for a new pure silver coin,
As good as any the rebel Carausius minted
For the first time since Diocletian came to power.

A new structure for the provinces, many subdivided,
Now grouped in dioceses, requiring more bureaucrats
For the Empire must be governed and governed well,
Which to Diocletian meant instructions in detail
Precisely given and properly supervised.

Among the provinces thus newly created,
There was one in Pannonia named for Valeria,
Just where the frontier river turns sharply south.
There Galerius had been campaigning when he heard the news
That Valeria had born him a girl child and all was well.

PROBLEMS ABOUND
throughout the Empire in spite of all Diocletian may devise

Durostorum

October
294
aet. 50

It hasn't changed, the sweep down to the river,
The marshes to the north stretch mile on mile,
The graceful herons, the tortoise on the road.
The fort at Durostorum is stronger now,
Like all the others rebuilt and reinforced,
The result of years spent strengthening the line.

At the brow of the hill the Emperor stops and looks,
Recalling memories, taking in the view,
Seventeen years since he commanded the legion here,
A third of his lifetime – so many years have gone.
Then all seemed possible and the strength was there,
He could ride for all the day, hardly an ache.
Now he prefers a chariot, even a litter;
At the end of a full day's ride, he feels his years.

From the fortress gate below, a trumpet calls,
The formal welcoming party comes in view,
The honour guard drawn from the Eleventh Claudia
And from the various cohorts of frontier troops.
The Emperor shakes himself, there is work to do,
No more time for dwelling on the past.
He canters down the road to inspect the guard.

A successful campaign completed against the Sarmatians,

DIOCLETIAN

The Emperor Diocletian with his imperial guard
Proceeds to winter quarters in Nicomedia,
Inspecting the frontier defences along the way.
He particularly wished to visit Durostorum,
As it was here that first he had been concerned
With the problem of how to defend the river line.

— * —

It is night on the second day, Diocletian stands
Watching the stars from the fortress bastion.
The day's work done, the defence review complete,
The sacrifice to Jove and the genius of the fort,
The latest batch of legal rulings given,
The delegates received from the veterans' colony,
The feast with the legionary officers and cohort commanders,
All done – and now the Emperor is alone,
Standing in the cool of the October evening
On the platform of the new bastion looking north,
Listening to all the night sounds from the river
Under the immense spread of innumerable stars.

A satisfactory day: the defences all are sound,
The frontier troops fully brought up to strength.
It was good to see the federates newly enrolled,
Saxons, Britons, Tungrians, Batavians, Gauls,
Safely stationed away from their lands of birth,
Mustered in cohorts along the river line.
The Eleventh Claudia were magnificent on parade;
The older men had served when he was there,
And doubtless now were boasting to recruits:
They knew the Emperor well, and called to mind
Incidents which proved he was a man and not a god.

The solemn sacrifice to the genius of the place
Had capped the day, had made him feel complete.
Returning here, he felt again the power
Which emanated from the very ground,
The shape of the hills, the way the river flowed,
The familiar sight of added man-made things,
Of roads and walls, of buildings and fortresses.
That each place has its spirit or genius,

PROBLEMS ABOUND

Strong or weak, depending upon who seeks,
Is a fact well understood by every man,
But it is a gift to be able to recognise
A place's genius and acknowledge it.

Quiet. The slight breeze brought the river sounds,
A boat approaching the dock, a muffled challenge,
An answering shout, a crunch, an oath and laughter,
Again the quiet and then the croaking of the frogs.
The half moonlight and above all else the stars,
Diocletian, the Senior Augustus, completely alone.

— ∗ —

Diocletian alone. To the north the barbarian tribes;
Every year more nations are coming out of the north,
Over the plains, across river and mountain range,
Navigating across the immense expanse of the steppes,
Piling against the frontier line in their hordes.
By rebuilding defences and increasing the army's size,
With constant vigilance the barbarians can be kept at bay.
So much for men, but what of their beliefs?

All can look at the stars, be they bond or free,
Man or woman, Roman or barbarian,
And see the immeasurable – but alone you see the stars,
No one else will see them precisely in a similar way.

Within the Empire, it is essential men should live,
Loyally in harmony in that station to which they are called,
Piously fulfilling all their obligations
To whichever place they be borne or pass their days,
So they can live in felicity, act well, and thrive
And ever enjoy the providence of the gods.
So it is necessary that through a religious act
Due acknowledgement be given to the order of the state,
Respect to the genius of the imperial house,
And to all powerful Jupiter, Father of the gods.

"When I, Diocletian, contemplate the stars
I see great Jupiter's work in the firmament.
How can I ensure that everyone also sees
The magnificent work of the Olympians in the night sky?"

DIOCLETIAN

The breeze blew from the river. It was suddenly cold.
The Emperor shivered, he shook himself and turned,
Leaving the bastion empty under the stars.

Christians, Beware

NICOMEDIA
DECEMBER 294
aet. 51

"How did it go?"
                "Not well. You know the man.
He was in one of his 'consultation' moods,
When he asks all and sundry for their opinion.
I sometimes think he does it to spread the blame
When he thinks he has an unpopular decision to make."

"But tell me what happened when you were called to dine –
It's not every day that you dine with the Emperor."

"I was given to understand the invitation
Was in honour of my recent appointment as governor
Of the newly created province Augusta Libanensis,
Carved out of Phoenicia at the recent reorganisation.
Therefore there was talk of Palmyra where he had served.
From there the conversation naturally turned
To the threat of Persia now that Narses rules.
The Emperor asked our opinion of the Manichees
And their religion, the latest to spew out of the East.
Were they really secret supporters of the Persian king?"

"And what did people say?"

                "There were present there
Many of us who believe the philosophers of Greece
Have discovered those secrets which have made the Empire strong,
And that the strictest observation of the religious rites
Honouring the Olympian gods is an essential part."

"Indeed. Indeed."

                "So we suggested the christians
With their secret meetings presented a greater threat."

"How did he respond?"

                "I think he is inclined
To agree with us, but he is very much averse

PROBLEMS ABOUND

To doing anything to upset the balance of the state.
He seems to feel the recovery is well in hand
But it is fragile and depends on confidence
Of ordinary people – and who knows what they believe?
There was some talk of looking at the stars,
And each man seeing them in different ways."

"What do you propose to do?"

"I have to return
To my province, for the Persian power is on the move.
The Caesar Galerius has returned to Antioch
And will be active on the frontier all next year.
With the help of the gods I will speak to Galerius
About the problems of this secret enemy.
I know the Caesar is inclined to the ancient gods,
And he is a man of action and not afraid
Of taking chances, when chances must be taken."

A Hard Day NORTH AFRICA
AD 295

The Proconsul was tired out and his wife knew it.
These recruiting tours should be a holiday,
That was the reason she had decided to accompany him,
But obviously today had been no holiday.
He had avoided her when the day's work was done;
Usually he came to her appartments and greeted her,
But today he had withdrawn to be alone.
So after due time she decided to seek him out.
She was concerned at this alteration to the usual pattern.
She would help him if she could, she wanted to know
What had happened that day to annoy him and make him so angry.

"Had one of those damn christians today. Such a waste –
Would have made a good soldier, certainly looked the part.
His father brought him but he wouldn't take the oath.
Tried to persuade him. Told his father to talk to him –
He said he was old enough to know his own mind!
I suspect he was a christian too. They're everywhere."

"But why did the father bring the son at all?"

DIOCLETIAN

"His job. He is responsible for getting the army recruits.
The legion here in Tebessa needs a new draft.
I really did try to persuade the lad, you know;
But it's essential the army always shows proper respect
To the divine Emperor, the eagles of the legion, and the gods."

"But what happened to the boy?"

                                      "Executed by the sword."

"What's happened to his body?"

                                      "The christians asked for it.
Taking it to Carthage, I wouldn't be surprised.
Make a martyr of him – Bad for discipline."

"And what of the father?"

                                      "He went away rejoicing.
Amazing! It seems he was happy at what had happened."

"And the mother?"

                                      "A mother? I didn't hear of a mother."

"There'll be a mother. There's always a wife or a mother."

A Mother's Lament

Why? Oh, why. Oh, why.

I sent out two this morning,
Proud, excited, my two men,
Hardly staying to say farewell
And now alone you come again.

They say your face, it shone with pride,
Self-satisfaction unalloyed.
Your Christ may have gained a servant
But for me, an aching void.

With mother's care I made new clothes
So the new recruit would do us proud,
His gift to the executioner.
I didn't sew to impress the crowd!

PROBLEMS ABOUND

I know you have to find recruits,
You have a job you must fulfil.
Our Maximilian would example set;
In others, discipline instil.

But stubborn are my two men,
You half guessed what he would do:
Refuse to serve, refuse the seal,
Acknowledge Christ in public view.

The Proconsul tried and tried again
To persuade our son so he could live,
Asked you to speak, to counsel him,
What saving help, did you then give?

All you could say was he knows best,
You left him there in his lonely state.
You knew he couldn't alone back down
But needs must a martyr new create.

I could not even have his corpse,
Your Christians had to have their Saint.
He has gone to Carthage, far away,
Despite my pleas and my complaint.

Writing this has helped a bit,
It's eased my anger and my pain,
But why dear Christ did you demand
My son. Oh why — explain — explain.

Beware of Bean Counters

"I don't like it. I don't like it at all.
Those census-takers count every blade of grass.
Nothing is sacrosanct, it seems, these days.
And they mumble about heads and yoke of oxen too,
I don't understand what they're on about
Except I am sure it will cost us an arm and a leg."

"Oh. I don't know. It is not as bad as that.
They have taken censuses for many years.
What's new is that they are now more businesslike,
As well as counting heads they are assessing land,

DIOCLETIAN

And reckoning what it will bear by way of tax,
Which means the tax demand is more fairly spread."

"I know all that, but the demand goes up and up.
Every year it seems it is more and more they need.
There are more legions, an increase in frontier troops,
More cavalry, more federates; many more than when we served.
They all need feeding. Soldiers seldom starve.
Have you ever heard of a tax demand reduced?"

"Oh. I don't know. It seems it is fairer now.
Before assessments and demands were arbitrary.
We can't remember it as we were serving,
But ask the old men, they'll leave you in no doubt,
The uncertainty of the system was a constant source of fear.
Now it's spread evenly and a regular annual event."

" But that's my point, it's a regular annual event!
Those nosey parkers from the Governor's office,
Mumbling about caputs and iugums, and looking for tips.
I don't like it. It's an invasion of privacy."

"But we are excused four caputs as veterans,
Having served our twenty years with the Claudia,
And even the men who left the legion early,
Providing the discharge was honourable, get some reprieve.
I'd much prefer a tax which one understands,
And pay it regularly, than the uncertainty of the past."

"But I'm told this method of assessing heads and land
Is only now gradually being introduced.
There are parts of the Empire which never have been taxed,
And other parts where groups have been exempt.
Mark my words, there is bound to be trouble there,
Where people are suddenly faced with a completely new tax.
It's all very well for our Lord, that great Quartermaster,
The divine Emperor, saying it is logical,
But it's not natural to be happy paying tax,
Particularly a tax which is new. It's not natural."

THE PERSIAN THREAT
and how Galerius is tempted and Diocletian responds with fierce determination

Valeria in Antioch

LATE 296
aet. 52

"I never liked Antioch much, least of all that year.
In spite of all the comings and goings at court,
I was desperately lonely. Galerius was on campaign –
The Persians had broken the peace and taken Armenia –
And I had just found out about Candidianus.
It was not that I objected to my husband's concubines.
There is not much point in objecting; it is a fact of life.
Men need women, and if I cannot give him a son
Then he naturally will try to get a son elsewhere;
But seeing the babe made me realise all that I'd missed –
I really wanted a son for Galerius.

My father, the Senior Augustus, had joined us there.
Having two courts in one palace is hard enough,
Not so much a question of precedence, that was never in doubt,
At least not in the minds of the staff of the Senior Augustus,
But just that there wasn't enough room for everyone,
And to add to this, my father decided to build!
He couldn't resist the temptation to build something anew
Whenever he saw a building which he could improve,
And the palace being on an island made matters worse.

And my mother, Prisca, had joined him for Saturnalia
I hadn't seen her for a number of years – she'd changed.

DIOCLETIAN

It seemed to me she had shrunk, turned in on herself,
Just as my father was growing ever larger and larger.
The court ceremonial had grown over the years,
Much of it based upon the Persian custom.
It placed the Emperor above all ordinary men,
A tendency not averse to my dear father.
But apart from the ceremonial, he was a great man;
He carried the ceaseless cares of our complex state,
He was the source of policy, the driving force,
Certainly helped by my husband the Caesar Galerius
And Maximian Augustus and his Caesar in the west
But in the end it was the Senior Augustus who had to decide
What was best for the well-being of the Roman state.

And I know this rankled with Galerius.
That year, he was almost as old as my father had been
When he had seized the purple on Numerian's death.
I know my father's authority lay heavily on him,
He yearned to be a great hero in his own right –
And I yearned for him, my fierce ambitious man.
When Narses invaded Armenia and broke the Peace,
Galerius leapt at the chance to prove himself,
So he had marched east before my father had arrived,
Collecting such troops as he could along the way.

Imagine my father's fury when he came
And found Galerius already on campaign.
Proper planning and preparatory work was his style,
Not risking all on a single throw of the dice.
He showed his displeasure when Galerius finally returned
In such a way that they made a ballad of it.
None of this made Antioch a happy place.

And then to add to this I had my Nurse –
Bless her! She prattled on, as if't were her right
Because she had known me long before I could speak.
Wisdom of the ages, she thought, I have no doubt;
Such jewels as 'I'd prefer one friendly word
However many provinces were named for me' –
Or – 'If he (she'd never give him a name)
Had only taken the trouble to be at hand
When the wee mite was born, all would have been well,

THE PERSIAN THREAT

And there would be many more babes for me to nurse' –
And on, and on but at least she was company.

But there was one advantage being in Antioch;
We were closer there to the eastern mysteries,
Born from the faiths of all those ancient nations
Ground down between the empires of east and west.
The christians, one of the newer Jewish sects,
Were well established here in Antioch.
A number of the palace officials and senior servants
Were followers of the way, including my dear nurse,
And for that I'll forgive her all her wise remarks.
It proved a help, that winter, in Antioch
Waiting for the Caesar Galerius to return."

The Ballad of Diocletian and Galerius   AD 296–297
aet. 52–53

Diocletian was a wily lord,
He ruled a vast empire,
But when he came to Antioch
He was full of ire.

All his plans for the Empire's good
Had been put to chance,
By Galerius his son
That his fame he might advance.

Now Narses King of Persia
Had broken the Peace,
And Galerius had rushed to fight.
That his prestige might increase.

Of all the schemes Diocletian had,
The greatest one was this:
He split the imperial power in four,
With the ultimate authority his.

His brother Maximian ruled the west,
Helped by Constantius.
Diocletian Augustus ruled the east,
His Caesar Galerius.

DIOCLETIAN

Galerius had gone to war,
With soldiers, far too few,
Hoping to triumph all alone,
And the other three outdo.

They brought the news to Antioch
Of the Persian victory,
How they'd pursued Galerius' men
As far as the eye could see.

Diocletian's anger was terrible
When he heard the news,
But then he thought most carefully
How he could this setback use.

For Diocletian was a wily lord,
Little he left to chance,
How to encourage Galerius
And the common good advance.

When Galerius returned to Antioch
Diocletian met him there,
Arrayed in purple in his chariot,
Imperious beyond compare.

Galerius approached on foot,
With his bodyguard,
Saluted his father respectfully
And met his stern regard.

Diocletian by his stern regard
Showed to Galerius,
He thought his action in this war
Both selfish and impetuous.

Now Galerius was a proud man too.
There he stood his ground,
Returning his father's fierce regard
Watched by all around.

They wondered who'd be first to move,
The father or the son.
They knew, here was a rivalry
Which had only just begun.

THE PERSIAN THREAT

It was hot outside the city walls,
But Galerius would not move.
It was as if by standing there,
His manhood he had to prove.

His father must ask him to mount
And show he was forgiven.
Diocletian waited for him to ask;
To this, they had been driven.

The watchers watched, the two men stood.
Neither showed signs of moving,
And people wondered what each of them
By standing there was proving.

Then from the watchers there was a sigh,
The chariot had turned around.
Therein Diocletian remained alone,
Galerius on the ground.

Diocletian rode to Antioch,
Saying never a word.
Galerius Caesar walked behind.
From the crowd not a sound was heard.

This continued for a mile
Before Diocletian waited.
Into the chariot he took his son,
His anger had abated.

You may ask the reason for this act
So unlike that wily lord.
He shamed his son for all to see
Instead of the usual accord.

Some say he planned it carefully,
That Galerius be inspired
To defeat the Persians once for all;
His ambition to this be fired.

The Persians were indeed defeated
By Galerius in the end,
But from that time there is no doubt,
With Diocletian, he did contend.

DIOCLETIAN

Diocletian may be a wily lord,
But it'll never be the same,
Since he made Galerius stand in the sun,
And we all saw his shame.

The Thirteenth Year

Antioch
AD 297
aet. 53

"Men say that numbers have significance,
Possessing a power, magical in themselves,
While some are lucky, others are of ill omen.
I'm not sure how far I hold to this belief,
But certain it was, that the time in Antioch
Was full of forebodings, setbacks and false alarms,
And the thirteenth year of my imperial reign.

So it was that spring in Syrian Antioch,
Galerius impetuously had gone to war
And as I feared, by Narses, been put to flight
Giving advantage to the Persian power,
Bringing disrepute to the family of Jove,
Just at the time when that of Hercules
Was riding high with Britain at last at peace.

Annoyance and fear ruled my thoughts those days,
Annoyance with Galerius and his selfish act
Of going to war alone to feed his pride,
And very real fear that all we had tried to do
Was now at risk, that we might not succeed.
Never before had I doubted our success,
In the end we would restore the imperial power,
But now with all the problems pouring in,
I found myself less sure. I slept with fear,
Fear which feeds on your strength in the dead of night.

Galerius, I brought to heel on his return.
I let him see my anger; he perhaps saw more,
Perhaps he saw my fear, but to the world
He accepted my paternal authority for all to see.
Determined to defeat Narses once and for all,
He has gone to Illyria to raise more seasoned troops.

THE PERSIAN THREAT

> Just as I began to feel we had turned the tide,
> With Narses held in check by the summer heat,
> News came from Egypt that the land was in revolt –
> I am told the new taxation is a cause,
> But I sense the hand of Narses and the Manichees,
> Their foul belief is spreading throughout the East.
>
> I must not allow this rebellion to succeed.
> One Domitianus has assumed the purple –
> We cannot afford another Carausius there –
> I must destroy this usurper and that at once.
> Action will drive out fear. We will succeed.
> How dare these little men stand in my way.
> We have work to do, an Empire to be saved."

Diocletian's Horse   ALEXANDRIA
AD 297
"Tell us the tale of the horse. Tell us again."   *aet.* 54

"But I've told you the story so very many times.
You must know it by heart, the tale of the Emperor's horse."

"But that's half the fun, having a story you know.
Go on. Please. Tell us the tale of the horse,
How the Emperor Diocletian came riding on a horse."

"Well, all right..."

                 The children settled down,
Securely anticipating a story many times heard.

"It was long ago and I was a young man then,
Living here in Alexandria, just as you do now,
But we felt different – Egypt was a special place,
Part of the Roman Empire, but still distinct,
More ancient than Rome with separate customs and rules."

They listened patiently as they always did.
This boring part would pass. They would come to the horse.

"I remember my father's anger when he heard the news,
That the Emperor, so many miles away, in his wisdom
Had decided to alter the way that we should be taxed.
No one was happy – the Alexandrians had always paid less,
A privilege won countless years ago,

DIOCLETIAN

This was cancelled. Now Alexandria would be like the rest.
And the rest were not happy, although they should have been.
The tax was meant to be spread more fairly throughout.
The people just didn't believe it, they knew they'd pay more.

So everyone rejoiced when they heard the call to arms.
The prefect was killed, we had a new Emperor,
One for Egypt respecting the ancient laws.
But then we heard the Senior Augustus had come,
The great Diocletian, awful in his power.
We waited with apprehension behind our walls."

And all the children listening drew closer together,
Familiar the tale, but nonetheless frightening.

"The cities fell to Diocletian, one by one,
Coptos went first, Busiris and Theadelphia,
Caranis and then Tebtunis, none withstood
The force of the mighty Emperor in his wrath,
Except for Alexandria – we were alone.

I remember those days as if it were yesterday.
We had all been enrolled in the special defensive force;
We were armed from the factories within the city walls,
And we held them back for there were not enough of them,
Alexandria was far too big, to lay close seige.
They cut the aqueducts, but we still hung on,
Day after day, we held them for eight long months.
Our leaders hoped the Persians would attack
And divert the attention of the Roman power,
But nothing happened in spite of promises.
The city defences were gradually ground down,
Hunger and lack of hope had had their effect,
And after eight long months we sued for peace."

The eyes of the listeners gleamed, now was the time,
They knew from experience, now was the time for the horse.

"There was a formal surrender. I saw it all myself.
The local defence force paraded without arms,
We witnessed Achilleus our leader bow down in the dust,
The keys of the city surrendered, all were laid low
Before the Senior Augustus, the great Diocletian,
There in his might, sitting high on his great war horse

THE PERSIAN THREAT

In front of the innumerable ranks of his imperial power
A sight impressive, most terrible to see.
You could feel his anger across the city square.

And the Emperor spoke, and a herald relayed his words
So all could hear, assembled in the square.
He spoke of the stubbornness of Alexandria,
How we had thwarted his divine intent,
Delayed the introduction of good new laws
Designed for the benefit of one and all.
For this we would be punished, so all would know
That foul rebellion never could succeed.
And he finished with these words, I hear them now:
'For this resistance you will pay with blood,
Starting with the soldiers paraded here in the square,
Your blood will flow in floods, in cataracts,
Blood enough to reach my horse's knees.'

On saying this the slaughter was put in hand
And in spite of pleas of mercy from all about,
The killing gathered pace, no let, the blood flowed free,
We unarmed soldiers were being hacked to bits.

And then a cry went up, but I could hardly see
From where I was pushed back against the wall,
But then I heard: 'His horse is on its knees!
We're saved. We're saved. His horse has fallen down,
The blood, such as it is, has reached his knees.'
Indeed it was so, and the sworsmen stayed their hand –
I could smell the sweat of the legionary nearest me,
They were as close as that when the Emperor's horse collapsed.
And then we heard the shout 'Hold your hands. Hold back.
The Emperor accepts the sign. There's blood enough.'

The children looked at their father with a sigh of relief,
And the older children wondered at the closeness of things –
If the horse had continued to stand just long enough
For the legionary's sword to make but one more slash,
Then... Oh! The closeness of things. The closeness of things.

"Later we erected a statue to the Emperor's horse.
We told the officials it was Bucephalus,
Our founder the Great Alexander's famous steed.

DIOCLETIAN

But we knew the subject was more contemporary,
As the name engraved on the pedestal made clear,
'Salvator' the saviour, which caused a considerable stir
Among our christian brothers, but we explained
It had indeed laid down its life for its friends."

Egypt Put to Peace

AD 298
aet. 54

"Well, how did he take it?"

"Not well. He looked a fool!
And Emperors are not accustomed to playing the part.
But he recovered himself quickly enough – that's a fact.
He observed that the fall of his horse was a sign from the gods,
And promptly called off the slaughter of the citizens,
But made sure their leader Achilleus paid the price,
Together with the others of Alexandria
Who had delayed for eight months the pacification.
They were formally executed in the city square.
There was no one who doubted our Emperor was in charge."

"What have we now to do with peace restored?
You were with the Praetorian Prefect for long enough.
Did he indicate what is on the Emperor's mind,
For sooner or later it will determine what we do,
We who sweat in the office of the Praetorian Prefect."

"I am not completely sure, but I can tell you this,
We are to proceed up the River Nile,
The Blemmyes are now to be dealt with, once and for all.
You know that their constant raids on the trading route
Between the Red Sea and Coptos on the Nile
Has long been a cause of legitimate complaint.
Well that is to be dealt with."

"But how are we going to do that?"

"I think they plan to settle the Nobatae,
The people presently living in Libya,
Put them between the Blemmyes and the frontier.
I know I have to draft a letter now
To the Governor of Libya asking his advice
On the present co-operativeness of the Nobatae."

THE PERSIAN THREAT

"But the land beyond the frontier in the south
Is hardly habitable. It is all rocks and sand."

"I think they mean to redraw the frontier line
So that the cataract at Elephantine
Is the southern point of full imperial power.
That's where we are now to go when things are fixed."

"But there is more afoot, of that I am sure.
Why all the coming and going of senior staff?"

"The Emperor has ruled that Egypt shall be divided
Just like the rest, with civil governors
And the army command kept separate – divide and rule!
So the top brass are coming eagerly looking for jobs."

"Anything else?"

"Well, there's something I don't understand,
I have a feeling it is important but I am not sure why.
The Praetorian Prefect was asking some local officials
To explain how the villages ordered their work in the fields.
You know how the flood of the river with its deposit of silt
Is critical to the Land of Egypt if the crops are to grow.
It is here for such a brief time and varies in height.
If the work is not ordered effectively and also with speed,
The villagers starve till the flood the following year.
Evidently the Emperor is interested in their method of work,
He's impressed the way the ordinary people are controlled –

But I have my letter to draft and you are to work
On the arrangements for the Progress south on the River Nile."

Seeing and Understanding   Summer 298
aet. 54

The screw turned,
 over it the peasant kneeled.
From the bank he watched
 the waters flooding the field.

The Emperor watched,
 from his seat on the barge of state,
The waters flow
 while the peasant manned the gate.

175

DIOCLETIAN

Great Jupiter
from his vantage could inspect
The two below,
determined they would connect.

The peasant turned
and saw the imperial barge,
A noble man
and the minions in his charge.

The Emperor saw
the peasant as he had ever been,
But he also saw
a cog in the state machine.

The Emperor knew
in this work done every hour,
He was witnessing
the basis of all his power.

THE GREAT VICTORY
**in which Galerius defeats the Persians
and together with Diocletian wins the Peace**

Diocletian Hears the News

PANAPOLIS
SEPTEMBER
298
aet. 54

" 'My Lord. Great News. A victory without compare.'
I well remember that day and the courier's shout –
I was in attendance on my chief, the Praetorian Prefect,
Being a junior officer on his personal staff.
(We were at Panapolis on the River Nile
Progressing north having settled the southern front.)
We were in the middle of advising the Emperor on the tax survey,
Which was gradually being introduced throughout Egypt.
The Emperor was speaking, saying we needed to know
Precisely who served in each village in the greatest detail,
Even unto the humblest worker of the archimedes' screw.
I was waiting for my chief to respectfully question our Lord
Why specifically he mentioned the screw, but we never heard –
The Master of Office was there, that I recall,
For the courier should have initially reported to him,
And not broken in without ceremony, in the way that he did.
The Master bustled forward but the Emperor stayed his hand,
And told the courier to present his important news.

This was something of an anticlimax, and proved the rule
That the Master of Office should first interrogate
All messengers and establish what is directly known,
For the man was but a relay and knew nothing himself,
Except what he had gathered by hearsay at fourth or fifth hand.

DIOCLETIAN

The Caesar Galerius had utterly routed Narses,
Put his army to flight and captured his baggage and wives.
It was when the Emperor asked for more details,
That it became evident that the man knew no more facts.
We had to wait for the despatches to be processed,
And I did not hear the details for another day,
But they proved a famous victory had indeed been won.

While we were travelling up the River Nile,
The Caesar Galerius with fresh Illyrian troops,
And his ally Tiridates, had attacked the Persians.
He had avoided the plain where he was defeated before,
Holding his force in the mountains of Armenia.
From there like a lightning flash, Galerius attacked
The Persian host when they were off their guard.
The Caesar Galerius himself acted as a scout
Choosing the moment when best to strike the blow.
Narses barely had time to scramble away,
Leaving his treasury, his baggage train and tents,
And what is more, his wives and concubines.
So confident of the outcome the King of Kings had been
He had brought his extensive family to see
A second victory over Galerius.
But our Caesar had learnt from his setback the year before;
With careful planning, daring and bravery he'd gained
A lasting victory over the Persian power."

Winning the Peace   LATE 298
                                aet. 54

"To the Noble Caesar Galerius, etcetera, etcetera.
Greetings from Diocletian Augustus unto his son.

With joy and admiration I received
The despatch announcing your great victory.
With Narses defeated and driven far away,
His wives and children seized, his treasure taken,
Together with many of his courtiers and men of rank,
You have gained an opportunity for Rome.

We have in these prisoners a powerful lever to hand,
To move the stubborn Persian power to yield.
For too many years their Empire has been a threat

THE GREAT VICTORY

To all our East, and now this can be fixed.

I will proceed to Antioch without delay
And be available there in your support.
Meanwhile can you inform me of your plans
Now that you have captured Ctesiphon.
I do not need to remind you of the fate
Of the Emperor Carus who ignored the Oracle,
And in spite of warnings crossed the fateful stream,
Only to be struck by lightning in the dead of night,
Lost in further Asia's vast expanse.

Can you also advise me where the prisoners are?
They are more valuable than all the gold
Which you have gained by your brave victory.
With them we will achieve a lasting peace.

From Diocletian Augustus, accept my good wishes. Farewell."

— * —

"To Lord Diocletian Augustus, etcetera, etcetera.
Greetings from Galerius Caesar unto his Father.

I acknowledge your despatch written at Panapolis.
Indeed we have an opportunity at hand.
The Empire of the Persians is undone,
Narses skulks in the extremities of the land.
Like the great Alexander I can seize
The whole of their Empire from here to the Indus shore.
The winter now draws on, a time to plan,
And in the spring I will campaign again.

I have lodged at Daphne the wives and concubines.
They are well treated as becomes their high estate.
They will be for us a weapon in the fight
To gain the Empire of the Persians once for all.

From Galerius Caesar, accept my duty. Farewell."

— * —

"To the Noble Galerius Caesar, etcetera, etcetera.
Greetings from Diocletian Augustus unto his son.

I have received your despatch here in Antioch.

DIOCLETIAN

I have just arrived ahead of the autumn gales.
Egypt is quiet, so we can concentrate
On making the most of your great victory.
The more I hear the clearer it is to me,
That in this the gods have given us the chance
Of finally settling the persistent Persian threat.

All that we four are struggling to achieve
Within the realm of Rome is put at risk
By the constant threat of jealous powers outside.
They see the lives our people now enjoy,
The fine cities, well tilled fields, the olive groves.
They see our citizens, each in their place,
Fulfilling their duties so all may benefit
From the increasing wealth, as our Empire lives at peace.
This peace is essential that our work may thrive,
For this we ever maintain the frontier line,
And by your great victory you have enabled us
To make the Eastern frontier inviolate.

I beseech you beware of Alexandrian dreams,
Of the tempting hope of conquering all the world.
Remember he died, and his empire died with him.
His generals and his courtiers each took their piece.
All that is left is the romantic memory.
Much better by far to build that which will last,
And this you have given us the chance to do.

I have sent my Master of Office to Daphne to see
That all is well with the wives of the King of Kings.
I will now proceed to Nisibis and await you there.
Let me hear from you with your plans as soon as you can.

From Diocletian Augustus, accept my good wishes. Farewell."

— ✻ —

"To the Lord Diocletian Augustus, etcetera, etcetera.
Greetings from the Caesar Galerius unto his Father.

I accept your advice in the matter of the eastern campaign.
My scouts reported the excessive distances
And the time it would take to reach the Indus banks.
I do not wish to be lost in those unknown lands

THE GREAT VICTORY

When I have won a victory which will set the seal
On our work here in the east for many years.

I will wait here in Ctesiphon, until I hear
That you and your court have arrived in Nisibis.
I will delay any further discussions with the Persian power
Until I have the chance to confer with you.

From Galerius Caesar, accept my duty. Farewell."

The Meeting at Nisibis   Spring 299
aet. 55

So they met at Nisibis, father and son,
The old man feeling older every year
But full of careful authority nonetheless,
The younger aware that the years were passing by,
Impatient to exercise full power alone.

It was the third hour, the spring sun warm on the back,
The wind from the Armenian mountains, blowing cool.
The Senior Augustus' legions stand on parade,
For the ceremonial meeting of their Lords.
The veterans recall the terrible time before,
When the Caesar in all his finery was made to wait,
Subject to the anger of the older man,
But now an outstanding victory has been won,
A triumph over the Persians, which at last avenged
The death of the captive Emperor Valerian.
All this achieved by Galerius, by him alone,
He comes as a famous general to Nisibis.

The Caesar Galerius was nervous in spite of himself,
He whose courage had been tested to the full,
When he had in person scouted the Persian camp
And chosen the moment to launch the surprise attack,
Caught them hemmed in, their battle line unformed,
Cut them to pieces with the Armenian horse,
He crushed the Persian splendour in the dust.

Nonetheless Galerius was nervous entering the square –
It was two years since that time at Antioch
When the Senior Augustus and he in ceremony met,
Two years since he had waited in the sun –

DIOCLETIAN

In parade dress and mounted, he fully looked the part,
A mighty general, a hero, a leader of men,
(And mounted he couldn't be kept standing in the sun).
He entered the square, where on other days merchants met,
At the far end he saw standing on the temple steps
Diocletian Augustus, formally in civilian dress,
Indicating thereby there was only one general that day.

Galerius dismounted and waited for his escort to form,
Then marched with precision across the market square.
Diocletian's troops acknowledged his victory,
The clash of weapons on shields, the roar went forth:
Caesar! Victor! Caesar! Victor!

He approached the steps, prepared his formal salute,
But the Senior Augustus was moving down to him,
"Welcome Victor of Narses. Welcome my son."

And so the two leaders embraced at Nisibis,
In the market square under the springtime sun.

The Persian Envoys Arrive

"They don't look like losers to me, that is a fact.
They were thoroughly thrashed but look how they're behaving now,
Proudly strutting in front of their retinue,
Behaving as if their Master owned the world."

"But they have come, that is what is significant.
No one was sure, you will remember, when Probus was sent
To persuade the Persian king to negotiate –
No one was sure, if we could make a deal.
It takes two to make a bargain and now they have come.
Evidently the King of Kings has certain needs
Which we are keeping in Daphne, close confined."

"You are on the staff of Secretary Sicorius Probus.
Tell me what you know of these fine fellows here
Who now we see entering the city square,
So full of confidence, as if they had won the war."

"The burly one, decked in dress uniform,
That is Barsaborus, their Commander-in-Chief,

THE GREAT VICTORY

A man of few words, but militarily competent,
Here I suspect to keep an eye on the other.
That is the thin one, tall, looking about,
Constantly looking for advantage – a man to watch,
That is the Lord Apharban, the Chief Minister,
The hand to the arm of Narses, King of Kings.
Indeed it is significant that he has been sent
To negotiate with our masters the fate of our worlds."

"Why significant?"

"Because it clearly shows
The King of Kings desires a firm accord
Which will last for ever, or for at least our time.
He has not sent a representative
Whom he can disown without great sacrifice.
He needs Apharban, and needs Barsaborus too,
He would not have sent them, if he were not serious."

The Negotiations   SPRING 299
aet. 55

[I am watching Galerius, listening to Apharban.
From where I sit on my throne, I can see his face.
Apharban continues stately phrase on phrase,
Galerius eyes half closed, he grits his teeth,
His colour's up but so far he stays his wrath.
Anger for sure has its place in negotiation
But too much can blur the message, all can be lost.
We have come a long way since the great victory,
Pray let not now all this be put at risk.
Great Jove intervene that Galerius be moderate –
But how this Apharban goes on and on...]

[I don't know how much more I can stomach of this.
I am amazed at Diocletian's determined patience.
He almost seems to be interested in Apharban –
How that man goes on – He started well enough,
Referring to the great victory and my part,
I admit I liked what I heard up to that point.
Then he was full of compliments about the way
We treated the prisoners at Daphne, and gave us thanks –

DIOCLETIAN

(As if civilized behaviour needed thanks!)
And now this Apharban goes on and on...]

"My Lords, your magnanimous treatment of your guests,
Close as they are to the heart of my lord the King,
Is an example to all of the way wise men should act,
For who knows when fortune's pendulum will swing,
Each day we witness happy men laid low,
Plague, sudden brawls, a slip, the fall of trees,
So many mishaps can change a person's life.
Therefore wise men when high on fortune's wheel
Are full of moderation, for they know
The wheel may turn and that most suddenly.
With confidence therefore we know that here we'll find
Moderation in victory from Rome's wisest men.

The Empires of Rome and Persia are twin eyes
Which illuminate the body of this world.
Whether men dwell in our empires or without,
All their lives are lit by these two eyes.
It would indeed be a sad disfigurement
If either eye be permanently put out.
A one eyed monstrosity..."

                       "Enough! Enough!"

[Galerius has moved at last. O may the gods
Inspire him with moderation, or all is lost.]

"Enough, You speak, Ambassador, of moderation.
But tell me, Sir, was moderation shown
When Sapor captured the Emperor Valerian?
What comfortable lodging then gave you your guest?
What food and medicines when your guest was ill?
And when he died, no proper burial,
You used the skin of his back to make a rug
To decorate the temple of your god.
Moderation indeed... [I feel Diocletian's eyes
Boring into the back of my neck. He wills me to stop.
Moderation indeed is what is needed now.]
You can be assured, my lord Ambassador,
No Roman needs advice on how to treat
A guest, whether he be freely invited or forced.

THE GREAT VICTORY

From the proposals we have prepared you will clearly see
Magnanimity is the watchword of our victory."

Diocletian relaxed – Enough anger but not too much –
The treaty was not at risk. They could proceed
To confirm by negotiation what they had won.

Thanksgiving

SPRING 299
aet. 55

Antioch-on-the-Orontes was in festive mood,
The Emperors had returned from the Persian war.
A formal triumph marked the victory,
Games in the hippodrome, all give thanks
With many sacrifices to the gods.

And now the most important of the sacrifices
The Senior Augustus and his Caesar make,
Before the new Palace entrance for all to see,
Acknowledging thereby the hand of Jupiter
In this great victory of our Roman arms.
The Emperors stand surrounded by their court
In their various hierarchies, rank on rank,
In front the crowd pushing to get a view,
Excited and happy to take their part that day.

There are many people witnessing the great event
But to everyone the gods give different thoughts,
To some it is a glorious spectacle
Fine to see but gone the following day,
In others deep religious feelings flow,
While others simply allow their thoughts to stray.

Among the women of the court Valeria stood:
"How our routines have changed with our Lords at court.
My mother pathetically anxious to please her man,
My father polite but distant in response,
And so my mother spends more time with me
When we are not in attendance on our Lords.
My husband, Galerius, I find subtly changed,
More confident now as Narses' conqueror,
Still given to fits of anger, frightening to see,
Less easily led by my father's authority,

DIOCLETIAN

But often I feel still led in spite of himself,
And that is when his anger seems the worst.

But my father, the Senior Augustus, has changed as well.
He seems to find it harder to exert his will.
He has to reason with Galerius and explain
The why and wherefore of every single act.
He seems to me old for the first time in his life.
I never thought I would see my father die.
They say he is essential to the state.
I know he has been essential in my life;
And now my man, Galerius, makes him less
By his very animal strength of being alive."

Further back among the court was Hierocles,
The Augusta Libanensis Governor,
A man of letters as well as a civil servant,
Well versed in philosophy, in Athens trained.
"It is good to participate in this sacrifice,
A confirmation of the old beliefs.
It is good to see our Imperial Leaders stand
And be seen by everone to be giving thanks
To the Great Jupiter for our victory.

But there must be many here who are christians.
That pernicious sect is strong in Antioch.
They even have in the city a theological school.
Would that all here were made to sacrifice,
The enthusiasm of the moment would carry many along
And loyalty would be shown to the ancient gods.

I know that the Caesar Galerius is keen to act
But the old man prevaricates, he is less sure.
He would prefer to leave them alone but they must not flaunt
Their refusal to acknowledge the Emperor in sacrifice.

We've made progress against the christians in the army, I hear.
They're tightening the rules relating to promotion and draft.
Adoring of the imperial image will be enforced
Both at recruitment and on the promotion parade,
As this includes the ceremonial scattering of ashes
The christians in the army will soon be ferreted out."

In the crowd a tall young man looked on with pride,

THE GREAT VICTORY

The pillared colonnade was the perfect set
For the fine ceremony of the victory sacrifice,
The morticed stone well cut, the fit exact,
Looked good to the professional eye of Zotikos,
Master mason and builder of palaces.
Proud of his three years' work, now unemployed,
He wondered what new task would come his way,
For a skilled man couldn't keep his family fed
On pride alone. He must pray for the Emperor,
That he be inspired with monumental thoughts
And dream of glorious palaces yet unbuilt.

AGAINST INFLATION
in which Diocletian attempts to defeat the greed of men

The Emperor is Concerned

ANTIOCH
AD 300
aet. 56

"The Emperor is concerned. Tell me, what are we to do?"
[And when the Senior Augustus becomes concerned,
It's advisable that every one is concerned as well.]
In the private office the four men sit alone,
They are the Emperor's senior financial advisors.
They have met together to agree how to respond.

It was the head of the Sacrae Largitiones who spoke –
He who deals with currency and public revenues –
He particularly addressed the head of Res Privata
Who is responsible for the Emperor's private wealth.
The other two wait and listen, the Praefectus Annonae
Who controls the Army's equipment, stores and supplies,
And the Master of Office, he who has to ensure
The careful running of the Emperor's bureaucracy.

"Our Lord the Emperor is concerned. You know what that means.
We had best present a common front, or else…"

"What precisely is his concern, and why at this time?"

"He was not, I fear, in his most communicative mood –
He was angry the way prices continue to rise.
Apparently he had seen a legionary ripped off,
The whole of his annual stipend used up at one go
Buying some worthless trinket in the bazaar.
How the Emperor saw this I am not precisely clear,

DIOCLETIAN

But certain it is that inflation is back on the agenda
As a prime concern of the Emperor and therefore of us."

"But the currency reform I thought had been a success."
It is the old Praefectus Annonae speaking now.
"It doesn't affect me much, as well you know,
Now that the army supplies are all in kind
And most of the soldiers pay is in clothes and food."

"The currency reform went well, I think I can say.
The new coin of purer silver was well received,
The copper nummus devalued, their issue increased,
But still the price of goods continues to rise."

"What's the effect of the more thorough land surveys?"
This from the Master of Office who is new in the job.

"Two that I know of," it is Res Privata who speaks,
"Firstly we now know more precisely what a province is worth
So the annona can now be collected efficiently.
The annual budget and the census' five yearly review
Are beautiful pieces of administrative machinery.

And secondly the landlords know what their estates are worth
And how many tenants they need to maintain that worth
Which results in people being kept tied to the land,
And the landlords know they must efficiently work the land
To fulfil their allocation and still have some to spare.
They have succeeded in this and the harvests too have been good."

The Praefectus Annonae breaks in: "Nonetheless they go up –
The prices of goods which the Army regularly needs."

"There are still so many in the world," another said,
"Who have to pay for things in current coin.
We are all being held to ransom by the merchants' greed
We have to think of ways of curbing them."

"We owe it to the ordinary people," said Res Privata,
"To make sure that prices remain reasonable."

"What is a reasonable price for a sack of wheat?"
There was a sudden hush. Each man looked at each other.
No one was able to answer the Master of Office.

"That is what we need. A list of permitted prices."

AGAINST INFLATION

Whose idea it was at first is far from clear,
But being trained as imperial bureaucrats,
They all considered the solution appropriate,
And what is more – likely to please their Lord.

More and more he preferred to solve problems with arbitrary rules
For persuasion and exhortation took far too much time.

The Edict on Prices   AD 301
aet. 57

The Emperors in their wisdom decided
An Edict on Prices be made,
That the continuous inflation
Should once and for all be stayed.

Diocletian, the Senior Augustus,
Commanded a line should be drawn.
The effect of the rise in prices
No longer could be borne.

So all the Emperors' servants
Travelled far and wide,
To establish every price
That inflation might subside.

The cost of corn was considered.
How much would a modius fetch,
Wheat and barley and millet,
Lupins, chickpeas and vetch.

Fermented drink was tested,
Both humble ale and wine,
Celtic and Pannonian beer,
Falernian and Surrentine.

Condiments were looked at,
Oil and vinegar,
Fish sauce and various salts,
And honey by the jar.

The list of meat extended
From pork and beef and lamb,
Through pheasant, and francolin,
To best Menapic ham.

DIOCLETIAN

The fish from seas and rivers
Were listed by scale and fin,
And oysters by the hundred,
Sardines and sea urchin.

Vegetables, nuts and fruit,
Radishes, gourds and turnips,
The largest African onions,
Palm shoots, apples and parsnips.

The finest olives from Tarsus,
Mulberries and Carian fig,
Firm-fleshed peaches and cherries
And mixed herbs by the sprig.

Wages were considered in detail
For every craft and trade,
The teacher paid per pupil,
The brickmaker by bricks he made.

The mason, the cabinet maker,
The layer of mosaic floors,
The wagonwright, blacksmith, the baker,
The carpenter of windows and doors.

The tailor for cutting the birrus,
The man who cleaned the drains,
What the scribe got for best writing,
And the bath keeper for his pains.

Leather and skins and hides,
Lasts for boots and shoes,
Sandals from Babylon,
And slippers of various hues.

Bridles complete with bit,
Halter with leading rein,
Saddles and cases in leather
Which five reed pens contain.

Then there was building timber
Priced according to size,
And loads of wood were listed
By carrier analyzed.

AGAINST INFLATION

Finished tools for trades,
A measure of one modius,
Vehicles of various sizes,
Some simple, others commodious.

Military equipment and clothes,
A cover to be used as a tent,
A soldiers's best quality mantle
And dalmatics of differing content.

Innumerable hooded cloaks
From Numidia to Britannia,
Silk embroidered shirts,
Mantles from Dardania.

Wages for those who prepared
The cloth and clothes they made,
The weavers and fullers, the sewers
Of beautifully embroidered brocade.

They assessed the cost of materials,
Raw silk of purple dye,
Wool dyed in various qualities,
And the prices which should apply.

Washed wool from different places,
Sea wool and rabbits' hair;
Wool from the Atrebates
Was assessed as the most dear.

Linen of the highest quality
And cloth of inferior worth,
And coarser linen yarn
For those of humble birth.

The finest shirts from Byblos,
They priced them by the web,
And cheaper ones from Tarsus,
The coarsest for slave or pleb.

Dalmatics, face cloths and wraps
From Scythopolis and Tarsus too,
And hoods, loin cloths and girdles,
Were considered in their review,

DIOCLETIAN

With bed linen and towels
And pillow tick from Tralles,
Whatever anyone used
From the greatest to the smallest.

Then they looked at gold,
Drawn out, in bars, refined.
They considered silver too
And to each a price assigned.

There were thirty one divisions
To this extensive list,
But things remained which analysis
Stubbornly did resist.

In the thirty second section
There were the bibs and bobs,
Like aluminium sulphate,
And materials for odd jobs,

Saffron, gum and mastic,
Wormwood and arsenic,
Oil of roses, first quality,
And myrrh Troglodytic.

The Emperors' servants returned.
The Edict was then prepared.
It was posted in all the cities
And maximum prices declared.

Everyone then expected
That prices would cease to rise.
In fact this did not happen.
They rose right through the skies.

They tried to enforce the Edict
Which increased the peoples' fears,
Benefiting one class only –
Historians in after years.

The People Speak

"But that's absurd! Only twenty a mile!"
The two men were peering at the lists posted in the square.

AGAINST INFLATION

"If I had to exist on twenty denarii a mile
On each of the wagons that I put out to hire,
There'd be no food at home – that's for sure.
My lady would have a word or two to say!"

"But I see here you can charge two denarii
For a man per mile to go with the wagon you hire,
So you can send two which'd improve your profit line."

"But here it says I must pay twenty-five
For a mule driver with his maintenance for a full day,
And three miles an hour is as much as you can expect
A wagon to do on an average working day,
So that is half the labour charge as an expense,
And you cannot count on full utilisation.
Whoever drew up this list knew nothing at all
About real life, and what happens in the market place."

"But if you read the edict itself it makes it clear
These prices are the maximum you are permitted to pay
So you can always pay your man a lower wage."

"I should be so lucky! Tell me, have you ever heard
Of a worker willingly accepting anything less
Than the maximum rate, especially when it's been posted
In every city square for all to see?"

"Perhaps the people drawing up the lists
Were not as foolish as you seem to take them for.
Look at the section dealing with army clothes;
The prices there seem lower than the civilian ones.
If we checked elsewhere, I think we would find this again.
That may be why the wagon charges seem low."

"You may be right. I shudder to think what's in store."

"Indeed there'll be trouble when they try to enforce these prices.
There'll be trouble throughout the Empire. Blood will flow."

"The trouble I shudder about is closer to home,
Some of these prices seem to me far too high.
What the old lady will say I really don't know –
A hundred for a modius of wheat – and for crushed beans!
I can hear her now: Absurd! Ridiculous!"

DIOCLETIAN

"Oh well! I just hope the Emperors know what they're doing.
But it seems unnatural to me to try to fix
Prices once and for all by a government edict.
The intentions may be noble enough but I doubt it'll work.
Why – by the time the edict's been carved on the wall,
The carver's own wages will be right out-of-date."

The Merchant's Tale

EGYPT
AD 302
aet. 58

"I like to think I influenced an Emperor,
(And I know I made a profit on the transaction too) –
That doesn't surprise you? 'Always do' you say.
The Emperor was the great Diocletian, the man himself.
To think I influenced the Ruler of the World.

It was the second time he came – the second as Emperor –
(I think he came as a young man long ago),
The first time he came as Emperor there was the seige,
The eight month seige of Alexandria.
His anger was terrible, his men were everywhere,
His time was fully taken up in settling things –
He had no time for antiquities on that occasion,
He had more leisure when he came the second time –
If you can talk of an Emperor ever having leisure.

I had heard that someone at court might want a sphinx.
You know how it is – commercial intelligence –
I had made the acquaintance of a young centurion,
He worked for the Master of Office, he knew him well.
I told my friend I was an expert in antiquities,
Not all that easy to obtain but I had a source.
He seemed to doubt me and I remember I got mad –
'I could supply the Pyramid at Giza – could supply the Sphinx.'

Imagine my amazement when I heard he wanted four!
My friend explained the sphinxes were not for him
But he had discussed it with his chief, the Master of Office,
And that high dignitary had in due course indicated,
He might be interested in obtaining four, if they matched.
I went to see him as soon as it could be arranged,
(It always takes time and costs money to deal with the court).

AGAINST INFLATION

He made it clear the interest was from a higher source.
I explained that sphinxes came in many sizes,
Could the higher source indicate to me the setting
As this would affect the size of the proposed purchase.
I emphasised 'purchase' more in hope than faith,
The higher the source the more likely the need for a gift,
A gift by me, a loyal servant of the state.

More waiting and then a message to be at court
At the time of Salutation the following day –
You know the custom how the courtiers salute their Lord
When he first appears at the breaking of the day –
I met my friend who led me to the Master of Office;
He greeted me, said we'd meet the higher source
And the purchase then might be clarified.
I looked around at the courtiers gathered there
Trying to guess which one wanted the sphinx.
It's strange to think I may have seen Constantine,
For he who was to be Emperor was there at the time,
Being groomed for the job on the Senior Augustus' staff.

The doors opened, the Emperor was revealed.
All of us bowed down in the presence of our Lord –
And even I, a trader, was impressed –
The Emperor moved gradually down the hall
As each saluted him, he acknowledged them,
Some well known to him – familiarly.
Those he did not know were named to him,
And he sometimes paused and would speak to them.

And so he came to us, we saluted him –
There is a formal wording which you use –
And then I heard the Master of Office speak:
'My Lord. Allow me to present Epiphanes,
One who is knowledgeable in antiquities.'
The Emperor stopped and looked me straight in the eye –
I remember thinking this man sees it all –
I realised I was face to face with the higher source –
Then I remembered I was a trader and went to work.

'My Lord. May I congratulate you on your choice of the sphinx.
The Egyptian sphinx, a lion with the head of a king,
The sign of royalty and of wisdom too,

DIOCLETIAN

Distinct from the variety which you find in Greece,
That is a mixture of woman, beast and dog.
To retain good fortune the two should be kept apart.'
(I was so nervous I hardly knew what I said
But I realised I had his interest. He was standing still.)

'Royalty and wisdom – that is why the sphinx appeals.
It is my desire to have four of matching size,
Not new hewn, but find me ones which hold
The ancient secrets of royalty and of strength.'

'If Your Lordship wishes, as I assume, to take these spinxes
To a foreign soil away from their natural home,
Then it's best to have a site completely new,
Or else the Sphinx's secret power is lost.'
(I had in mind that with an empty site
I could supply sphinxes of any size.)

'I have such a place in mind. It's across the bay,
(I saw the Emperor there beside the Nile
Smiling to himself and looking far away.)
Sheltered from the sea the thorny aspalathos grows.
There the sphinxes can keep their secrets safe.'

The officials were getting impatient. The Emperor turned
To acknowledge the salutations down the line.

How did I influence the Emperor, I hear you ask.
To my certain knowledge, that was the very first time
The Emperor spoke of the place where he would retire.
I was the one who suggested it must be new –
As new as the thought that an Emperor could retire,
And new so my sphinxes might be of any size.

And what of the sphinxes? I found them in the end –
Genuine pieces more than a thousand years old.
I am told they are set up round the Mausoleum.
I heard this from Zotikos, he is the man in charge.
I have the contract to supply antiquities.
They have many columns from Egypt, I am proud to say,
But not as proud as the fact that the Emperor
Chose the site for his retirement palace because of me."

AGAINST THE CHRISTIANS
**in which Diocletian is persuaded to make
the Christians conform**

Diocletian Dreams Again LATE 302
aet. 58

I saw the man again, the man with the loaf –
Not clearly, but it was definitely the man with the loaf of bread.
In the past few months I have seen him more than once,
But more clearly now than it was at the other times.
I recognised him – I wasn't sure before.

You know how in a dream you see with more than your eyes –
You sense the whole aura of a person and your feeling too.
Sometimes only as the dream is seeping away
Do you recognise with certainty that person's daytime body
And you know you have seen right into them utterly.
So I recognised the man with the loaf of bread,
Though his daytime body was in a dream long since gone,
Lost somewhere in the furthest crannies of my mind.

It's a relief to know it's the man who's been in my dreams.
It brings some order to the private world of sleep,
That uncontrolledly laps around my bed
With ill defined and disproportioned fears.

How different these dreams from the one so long ago –
That was clear cut, that much I can recall.
That dream Great Jove and Hercules made plain.
Now nothing is clear, just glimpses of the truth.

DIOCLETIAN

So it was last night when I recognised the man.
I was on the sea shore far away in Gaul –
Why Gaul? I hadn't dreamt of Gaul for years,
But I knew it was because the tide was out.
The sand lay dry as far as I could see,
Something you never witness in the Inland Sea.
All seemed set fair but there was something I had to do –
I had to build a wall but had only my hands,
And the sand, it stretched as far as I could see.
I began to dig and Galerius was digging too –
He turned, grew larger, his face was full of scorn,
He looked at me with fearsome wild eyed hate.
He shouted something pointing to the sea,
And as the tide swept in, I saw the man
Struggling there in the waves, he looked at me
And the look…

                    …I am not sure — and then I awoke.
And all I know, is that I have to know
What the man with the loaf of bread had meant by that look –

Terrified, betrayed but also understanding.
And in spite of my lack of knowing, I know this –
I must work for the man however strong the tide.

But Jupiter, I'm tired, help me with all this sand.

The Emperor Passes

BITHYNIA
LATE 302
aet. 58

"Look here they come! I am glad you said we could watch.
What a chance to see Our Lord the Emperor."

"You may not actually see the Emperor himself.
I didn't, the only other time I had the chance,
But I saw the Emperor, our present Lord I mean.
He was commanding officer of the Protectors then.
But all we saw of the Emperor was a litter."

"I hope we do better than that. We have come a long way.
I told everyone else I was going to see the Emperor.
There is the advance guard. Oh they are marvellous!"

"They certainly look the part and they certainly should,
Considering all the taxes we have to pay

AGAINST THE CHRISTIANS

To keep the army in place and fully equipped.
They are smarter than when I saw them years ago."

"How can you remember, Father, as well as that?
It must be more than twenty years since then."

"All that I can really remember is my Uncle saying
They had been smarter in Aurelian's days!
But there is no doubt our Armies win their wars,
The Persian power has firmly been put in its place,
All the barbarian nations attacking from the North,
Conquered or kept at bay by our Emperors.
We do get value even if we have to pay."

"I can't see the Emperor, Father. What can you see?"

"There is the baggage with the escort. He will come next."

"It is a litter. Not anyone on a horse.
All this way and there is no Emperor.
What am I going to say when I get home?"

"That you saw the greatest Emperor we have known
Riding past in a litter, for he is tired –
Tired with the many concerns essential to our state.
You cannot expect him to show himself every day
So boys can boast they saw the Emperor.
What I know is we can leave the farmstead safe
When we come to see the Emperor on an outing like this.
Last time we hid the stock on the summer steading.
But now there is a proper regard for the law."

"But I wish I had seen the Emperor himself."

"I am sorry too. It doesn't seem good to me.
Last time the Emperor was imprisoned in his litter
He never came out alive – and now we have this.
I trust this doesn't prove to be an augury."

A Long Winter   AD 302–303
                       aet. 58–59

There was no rest for Diocletian in Bithynia;
All winter long Galerius and he conferred,
Closeted alone in the palace, while outside
The wildest rumours were all that people heard.

DIOCLETIAN

The Senior Augustus came to Nicomedia,
Seeking his Caesar's advice and his support,
How best he should complete his twenty years
And the restoration, for which they all had fought.

The Caesar Galerius came with a different aim;
The christians must be utterly eradicated.
While people failed to honour the ancient gods,
The work of restoration remained frustrated.

Great Jupiter observed this clash of human wills
On which the fate of the Olympian gods depend;
One all raw and strong, the other old,
There in Bithynia god watches them contend.

— * —

"Are they still there?

    "Well certainly the Praetorians are.
They only guard the palace when the Emperor is there.
It's certainly true we haven't seen either of them –
They must be closeted there without their advisers."

"But what do you suppose they're spending the time discussing?
This isn't the way they usually behave when they are here.
No gathering of friends and advisors, and ordinary business.
I wonder what it's all about?"

    "A new campaign?
The Persians hardly need another lesson,
But the Carpi and the Sarmatians are always there
Waiting to be taught the facts of Roman life."

"I heard that another form of tax is planned.
Maybe that is what the discussions are all about."

"I cannot say I like it when our Masters behave
In a different way from usual. It is ominous –
You can be quite certain they are not discussing the races
And giving each other odds on the Blues and the Greens."

"Oh. I wouldn't worry too much. The Old Man is all right
He will keep an eye on things. He always does."

"But that is the point – the Old Man is old indeed.
I saw him when he arrived. He certainly looked his age –

AGAINST THE CHRISTIANS

They almost had to carry him out of the litter.
I haven't seen the Caesar but I am told
He looks fighting fit and is always raring to go –
I wouldn't like to be a Sarmatian in his way…"

"…or a tired old man. Is that what you are saying?"

"Well, shall we say I would prefer to have the head
Of the older man, on the young man's vigorous body.
Let us hope their deliberations have this effect."

— ✻ —

"It's over three years since I saw my Mother and Father,
More than three years since we were in Antioch.
What a change there seems to be in both of them.
I remember thinking then how she'd been reduced,
Shrunk and turned in on herself, but look at her now –
Now my Lady Prisca is completely drained,
As if the living at the imperial court
Has proved too much for her – she is all used up.
I hope we have the time this winter to talk
And revive the friendship we had when I was young.

And in my Father I see a change as well.
When I was young he was indomitable,
Constantly seeing round the edge of things,
Making connections obscure to other men,
He dominated by the strength of his intellect
And by his determination to achieve.
Now that he is older, he tires more easily,
He finds it harder to exercise his will,
More easily frustrated, more often given to anger.
It is as if the task of restoration,
The task he set himself has sucked him dry.

The Caesar Galerius, fierce and strong in his powers,
A man I know well, to whom I am proud to be married,
Comes here hot foot from the bloody barbarian wars,
Eager to be recognised for what he is,
The champion of the ancient faith and the Olympian gods.

And why am I telling you this? Because I care –
I care for these two men who are close to me,
I care so much that I want you in after years

DIOCLETIAN

To know about them and care as much as me.
Men talk about the great political shifts
Which we are witnessing in these troubled times,
But I am concerned about these men I know.
It is they who are important and that is the reason why
I tell you this, that you may remember them
As ordinary men caught up in the web of life."

— * —

Flaccinus, newly appointed Praetorian Prefect
Was frankly excited by the meeting that had taken place.
The Master of Office considered his longer service
Justified a more world-weary knowledgeable air.

"Well, what do you make of that?"

"It was quite a scene!
I have seldom seen two people further apart
Who believe they have a common aim in view.
I felt uneasy after the first exchange."

"How's that, Prefect? That seemed normal to me."

"The Vicennalia was on the Augustus' mind.
You know he wants to celebrate in Rome
But Caesar Galerius will remain here in the East,
And the Chief is concerned to have his agreement to this.
There is only a year to go and it does take time
To organise a celebration of suitable size."

"I think, Prefect, the fact that a number of triumphs
Which they will celebrate, were actually earned
By the Noble Caesar Galerius – I think that hurts."

"So our Chief begins to speak of the Vicennalia
And says he wants the Noble Caesar's advice –
I was shocked as well when the Caesar interrupted,
Saying there was business which needed to be completed
Before the twenty years could be celebrated."

"But Prefect, the Caesar Galerius has always interrupted.
He listens in the end. You just wait and see."

"Yes, but I was surprised at the fierce intensity
With which the Caesar then drove home his point.

AGAINST THE CHRISTIANS

I knew, of course, his concern about the christians,
But I had not realised how strongly he held the view
That the followers of this cult have been the cause
Of all the afflictions which have befallen us.
I was surprised when the Emperor didn't at once agree."

"I think, Prefect, we are in for a long winter!
The Caesar is determined the ancient gods will be served;
The Senior Augustus is very much aware
That our great Empire rests on a delicate balance.
He fears that if he follows the Caesar's advice,
The balance will be disturbed and everything lost."

Dinner Talk

Another afternoon in that long long winter,
Another dinner with Galerius as the host,
The Emperor Diocletian half listens, he plays with his food.
He looks at the guests the Caesar has asked to dine:
Sossianus Hierocles, the Governor of Bithynia,
A leading light among the Platonists
Together with a number of other philosophers –
[Evidently the Caesar plans an intellectual attack.]
Lucius Flaccinus, the new Praetorian Prefect,
Fast learning the ropes of his trade and where the power lies,
Veturius, Master of the Soldiers on the Danube front –
[Let us hope the Barbarians this winter stay safely at home.]
There is Priscillianus another of Galerius' friends.

The Caesar Galerius watches the old man as he looks,
[Let the others speak, let the pressure be indirect,
But wear him down we will. The gods will be served.]

"...Ever since the christians have been upon the earth,
The world has gone to ruin, nature is decayed."
So another of the Caesar's guests droned on and on –
"The celestial beings themselves have abandoned us,
Giving up that care which hitherto they used
To watch over the interests of the human race.
The gods have been banished from every part of the earth –
All this has happened since the christians have been with us."

[But our temples are forsaken, the shrines unkept,

DIOCLETIAN

The fault lies not solely with the christians.
But I will hold my peace for words in such company –
Words with wine can so easily mislead –
The decision is far too serious that we have to make.]

"The earth is in decay," another chimed in,
"The massive invasions made by the Germans and Goths,
Which your noble forebears Probus and Claudius fought,
Could not have been contemplated in the ancient times
Before the christians spread within our lands."

[But the forts, the strong points, and the defence in depth,
That is what keeps the barbarian tribes at bay.
Little or nothing to do with the christians.]

Then another, [Great Jove – how they go on!]
"Now with utmost effort our defences hold,
But decay continues, famine, drought and plague –
Locusts devour the crops, and mice the corn –
These frightful things are inflicted on all of us
By the gods exasperated by these christians."

[I think that locusts and mice were there before Christ
And men found others to blame in the ancient times.]

"I find it extrememly difficult to understand,"
Now Hierocles was speaking [A man worth listening to]
"How these christians dare to worship an ordinary man,
And a man condemned to death – crucified –
A death which would shame the very lowest of men.
Divinity cannot be touched by violence
And yet these christians hold to the belief
That this god of their's died a violent death."

"And their language!" another spoke, "It's barbarous –
The Greek they use is vulgar."

                      "You can't believe
The story of their Christ. They were common men
Who claimed to know him alive in Palestine –
Not reliable witnesses, not honest men."

"What I can't understand" [they are excited now]
Why the christians behave so exclusively. They cut themselves off.
If these men really had holiness in their hearts,

AGAINST THE CHRISTIANS

They would honour all of the other gods as well.
They seem to behave as a state within the State."

"They deserve our hate the way they spurn our gods.
We honour all the gods, each city's gods,
The genius of every place, for they all lead
To the Supreme Godhead which all men need to worship."

"And tell me this. What happened before their god?
Are you telling me that all men died in vain?
It's only three hundred years since they made their god.
Was everyone before completely mistaken and fooled?
That I certainly cannot believe. It's all too new –
Men's need to worship goes back much further than that."

The Caesar watched. The Senior Augustus frowned –
This constant talk of the christians tired him out.
[There'll be more tomorrow if Galerius has his way.
I would be alone to think, away from this talk,
And then to sleep, but not dream of christians.]

— ✻ —

At last I am alone with time to think;
These constant meetings are exhausting me.
I need to know what still has to be done,
Before we can celebrate our twentieth year.
The gods have blessed our reign, they've given us time
To restore the fortunes of the Roman state.
It is meet and proper that I complete the onerous task
And ensure that all our people remain at peace,
But Galerius only talks of christians,
And this has affected all our entourage.
Nowhere can I turn but there is talk of christians.

I cannot believe a cult a few hundred years old
Can compare to the ancient truths of the Olympians.
I cannot believe the Supreme God waited so long,
And I cannot condone their refusal to sacrifice
Thereby refusing to acknowledge our authority –
But normally they live quietly observing the laws.
These christians seem to have a habit of dying gladly for their faith,
So I fear that insisting our christian subjects conform
Will cause such great discord throughout the realm

DIOCLETIAN

That all we have struggled to achieve will be set at nought.

I have used these arguments again and again,
But I find Galerius constantly returns to the question.
Gone is the time when I only needed to nod
And everything happened exactly as I desired.
But now I have to justify all my thoughts,
Explain my fears and argue incessantly,
Repeating arguments until I am not even sure
I believe what I am saying is anywhere near the truth.
Great Jupiter knows it is the truth I seek.

Consulting the Oracle   Early 303
aet. 59

After weeks of deliberation Diocletian acts –
Apparent action but still the decision deferred.
He calls a council that he may take advice
How best the Imperial Government should deal with the threat
Posed by the followers of the christian cult.
Following the age-old custom he summons his Friends,
His officials and advisers, he questions everyone
From the least through to the senior, he sounds them out.
He sits there, inscrutable, carefully weighing their views.
Beside him sits the Caesar far from inscrutable;
He looks with favour on those who counsel force,
Fearfully he glares at those who would mitigate
Strict application of the Imperial Power –
Moderation is discounted, it is action that is required.
Galerius smiles grimly, Diocletian contemplates.

The Senior Augustus announces his decision –
And yet it is no decision, he still delays.
He decides it would be best to consult the gods.
He will send his haruspex to the Oracle
To consult the god Apollo at Didyma.
The Senior Augustus rises, the council adjourns,
The Caesar Galerius grimly sweeps from the hall.

— ❋ —

"Quick. Come here."

                     "Yes. What can I do for you?"

AGAINST THE CHRISTIANS

"You know, I think, the citizens of Miletus well.
You have cousins there if I remember right."

"Indeed I do, my father's younger brother
Had four sons in the evening of his life.
Two have done well, the others I'm not so sure –
These two reside in Miletus and are counsellors.
They are held in high regard…"

                                "I have no doubt.
Know this. The Emperor sends to Didyma
He wishes to consult the Holy Oracle."

"Then no decision was made at the council after all?"

"None, except this, that he would consult the Oracle.
He sends the Haruspex and counsellors,
Escorted by the noble Tribune Constantine.
Now through your friends at Miletus can you find out
Who serves as priest this year at the Oracle,
For the council of Miletus traditionally provides the priests
And has its share of the dues from Didyma?"

"Certainly that can be done."

                                 "Then you do this.
Give him this message, it's brief. Have him learn it by heart.
It will help him interpret the message Apollo shall give."

"It shall be done. It is an honour to serve the cause.
These christians grow too proud. They are everywhere."

"Good man. Go saddle your horse. There's no time to lose.
The Emperor's men will set out this very hour."

— ✳ —

        Apollo of Didyma, we cry to thee
        Show us the future that lies in store.
        Apollo allow us plainly to see
        What is to come as clear as before.

        Inspire your servants to prophesy
        The truth that all can understand,
        A message on which all can rely
        With confidence in every land.

DIOCLETIAN

    May the sacred spring freely flow,
    Wash the priestess' robe and hem.
    Let her breathe the scent that she may know
    The truths from which tomorrow's stem.

    And may your priest truly explain
    All that the inspired priestess shall see,
    So everything is then made plain,
    Apollo of Didyma we cry to thee.

— ✳ —

From the outer court of the temple,
          awestruck they peered down the stairway,
The moaning cry of the priestess
          echoed from below eerily,
The sun suddenly was hidden
          by the clouds, all was quietness,
Nervously they waited for the priest
          of Apollo to interpret the message:

"There is an obstacle to Apollo telling truth
          to his servant the Emperor.
It is the righteous who dwell on the earth
          who prevent the god speaking."

Diocletian Receives The Answer

    [From where I sit I can see it all,
    The Praetorians and the Protectors standing guard,
    The Counsellors ranked according to their degree.
    How many times have I witnessed such a scene
    Since the days when I stood guard for Aurelian.
    But none had greater decisions to take than this,
    How I wish I felt more certain how we should act,
    I feel that I feel and not what I should do.
    My tiredness makes me think about myself,
    Instead of concentrating on the task.

    A trumpet sounds, then enters the Haruspex
    With the party led by the Tribune Constantine,
    Whom we sent to consult the Oracle at Didyma.
    They approach the throne and bow in unison.

AGAINST THE CHRISTIANS

I can feel the suppressed excitement in the hall,
None more than the throb of physical power at my side,
The Caesar Galerius sits forward on his seat,
As one who watches a duel in the amphitheatre.]

The Master of Office opens the proceedings and says:
"Honoured Haruspex, I call on you to speak.
The Senior Augustus and the Noble Caesar require
To know the message from the divine Apollo.
He who sees the future, what does he say,
What is the message from the Oracle at Didyma?"

The trumpets sound again, the Haruspex bows,
Moves forward, and his measured answer rings out clear:

"There is an obstacle to Apollo telling truth
                             to his servant the Emperor.
It is the righteous who dwell on the earth
                             who prevent the god speaking."

And he said no more. The court was utterly quiet.
Then a gasp and whispering and muttering and looks askance.

[I must speak before formality all dissolves:]
"What means this message from the Oracle?
Who are the righteous that are the obstacle?"

Even then the priests who were with the Haruspex
Kept silent, each fearing to be the first to speak.
The silence continued, the tension further increased.
A voice from among the priests at last was heard:
"It's the christians who call themselves righteous, they are the ones
Who present the obstacle to the god telling the truth."

There is a sigh in the hall, tension drains away.

[I know I must act, no longer can I delay.
My Caesar, my council and now the god himself,
All have told me to act against the cult
To complete my work of imperial restoration.]

"It is essential that the christians now conform."

DIOCLETIAN

Bishop Anthimus

Bishop Anthimus sat alone in front of the hearth.
It was a cold day; the wind blew in from the sea.
It had been a long winter, there was no end in sight.
The rumours from the Palace made it seem colder still,
The Bishop's rheumatism was worse when the news was bad.
Earlier, when the Senior Augustus had just arrived,
Their friends in the Palace had suggested all would be well.
The Emperor had spoken of the need for calmness and peace.
But now the Oracle of Didyma refused to speak,
And the Christians were directly blamed for this disaster,
And the wind was cold and the joints of the Bishop ached.

But would the Emperor finally act? All had been quiet
For more years than most of them could call to mind.
Anthimus was a youth when the last persecution ceased
And the Emperor Gallienus had ordered their property restored.

And did they feel threatened, the community in his care?
He thought of his congregation at the Eucharist
The ladies of fashion, those of lower degree,
The slaves, the servant girls, the prostitutes.
Why dear God did he think of the women first?
Keep my thoughts from straying sinfully.
However much the deacons at the door
Tried to control and catechise this half
To ensure no one with heretical views got in,
Scandal still was caused by evangelism
By ladies with a personal idiosyncratic view,
And as for dress... dear Christ pray give us strength!
At least they have by tradition to sit at the back.

And what of the other half, what of the men?
They have their subtle signs of dress as well
Which indicate to their fellows their degree,
And if I notice this, where are my thoughts?
Keep me, dear Lord, from the sin of frivolity.
But what of these two halves, are they concerned
We may have to choose between the everlasting life to come
And life tomorrow in this life we know so well.
God give us strength to know the life to choose.

AGAINST THE CHRISTIANS

How have we come, after years of peace, to this?
There are followers of the way throughout the land,
In Nicomedia there're Christians in every walk of life,
On the Emperor's private staff, teaching in schools,
Many in the Army still in spite of new rules.
I think we've been deceived by the apparent ease
Of the last few years. We have fallen prey to sloth.
'We will progress', we said. 'All will be well.'
With sloth came pride. 'Progress is ours by right!'
Intolerance followed pride, we fought together,
Argued about the minutiae of our faith,
Arrogantly dismissed our brother Christians as fools,
Built fine new buildings, like the church here in the square,
Which casts its shadow across the palace tower,
Built in our pride for this world, not for the next.

What should I do as leader of this flock?
Stand or run? – Thy will be done, O Lord.
Standing firm sounds fine but who will then tend your sheep?
And a Bishop standing firm the powers can see.
Martyrdom is glorious but it is also absolute –
Can more good be done with the time that running earns
In all those years until one's natural death?

It is absolute indeed – all then will end,
No more time to sin, or to confess,
No more the opportunity to get it right.
But no more time for the difficulties of the work:
The confessors who have suffered for their faith and lived,
Their authority within the flock a rival source –
The soldiers dismissed for refusing to sacrifice,
Claiming virtue thereby, brazenly ignoring our word –
Those of the presbyters who were here before,
Who speak of the wisdom of bishops in earlier times –
And no further need to be concerned with cash,
No need to discern the source or decide its use –
No more time for religious argument,
No more letters, no further sermons to give.
Absolute release but absolute judgement too,
I am not ready for that, God knows that I am not!

DIOCLETIAN

And with more time there is still so much to do,
The newcomers to be taught and then to be baptised,
The deacons trained, prepared to be presbyters,
A final choice be made of the next in line,
So our people have a worthwhile candidate;
A few more years, all then will be prepared.

There is no time, now is the moment of choice,
The sword is about to fall upon the church.
I must act – and being a sinful man of clay
I will start at home with my children and my wife.
It would be as well if they go to the countryside.
The government's writ runs less thoroughly there.
Philomena can visit her sister and take the boys.
I hope she feels the inconvenience of the country visit
And her forbearance with her sister earns for her
Rewards out of all proportion in the life to come –
Our God moves in a mysterious way indeed –
Thinking of her sister's family makes it clear
I have to stay alone in Nicomedia.

Now for the organisation of the church,
Half of the presbyters should now depart.
I must ensure that includes some of the younger ones.
There will be a need of shepherds for the scattered flock.
The teachers such as Lactantius and Lucian
Can look to themselves, they have the intelligence
To judge what may happen and then know what to do.
That will leave five of the elders and myself –
Thy will be done O Lord. Thy will be done.

Now to the most difficult part – there was a draught in the room,
The fire had gone out in the hearth, the cold wind blew –
"Philomena where are you? I have something to consult you about…"

Terminalia

NICOMEDIA
MARCH 303
aet. 59

First light of day at the Feast of Terminalia,
The cold wind blew in from the wintry sea,
The Praetorian Guard paraded in the city square
With the Prefect, financial officials and engineers.
The Augustus and Caesar looked on from the Palace tower.

AGAINST THE CHRISTIANS

The ordinary people idly watched the show,
Possibly a new parade for Terminalia.

Galerius looked grimly down – an auspicious day,
The Feast of Terminus, the ancient boundary god,
Dedicated to the final end of all the christians! –
Diocletian was equally grim. They must conform!
The edict had been carefully drawn to that effect –
But the Senior Augustus insisted no blood should be shed.

The Guard advanced in order across the square,
The engineers equipped with axes, crowbars and pikes
Surrounded the church waiting for the signal to start –
No fire was used for fear that it might spread –
A trumpet call, the soldiers attacked the church,
The proud and lofty building soon came down,
The holy books were burnt in the city square.
The Emperors retired to dinner, the day's work done.

On the following day the imperial edict was posted –
All places of christian worship should be destroyed,
All holy scriptures committed to the flames,
Christians no longer might meet to worship their god,
All those who persisted in adhering to the christian faith
Would be deprived of official position and rank,
Would lose all legal status in the courts,
Be subject to torture whatever their rank might be.

Immediately from the crowd, a man ran out shouting,
He tore the edict down, waving it about,
Asking if this was yet another proclamation
Of the umpteenth victory against the Sarmatians and Goths!
He was arrested, hustled away and put to the torch,
Roasted according to the strictest process of law,
And finally burnt in a glorious martyr's death.

So Euethius was the first to die. The Emperor was right –
Christians in truth had the habit of dying gladly for their god.

— ✶ —

DIOCLETIAN

Thunder at night and the lightning,
Briefly all is revealed,
The windswept sea and the promontory,
Then darkness and all is concealed.

The sudden spring storm and the high wind,
A boat is caught unawares,
Buffeted in the bay by the breakers,
Struggling as the rockface nears.

The men in the boat are despondent,
They call on the gods and they cry.
Lightning and the world is exploding,
They give themselves up to die.

As suddenly the storm has departed,
In the east the glorious Sun.
Calm as the boat makes the harbour,
The newborn day has begun.

Jupiter Intervenes

Great Jupiter was concerned with what he saw,
The followers of this new god from the east
Survived in spite of all his servants did,
And everyday their influence increased.

To Jupiter it seemed, Diocletian worried more
That order throughout the imperial realm prevailed,
Than that his people worshipped the ancient gods
With all the benefits which that entailed.

What use an edict which only destroyed the shell,
Brought down their holy places, their scriptures burnt.
The people themselves must fully be put to the test
That Jove's omnipotence is everywhere clearly learnt.

Great Jupiter looked with favour on Galerius,
He was a man not frightened by having to act.
How could Jupiter encourage the older man
With that fierce consuming certainty he lacked?

AGAINST THE CHRISTIANS

Jupiter raised his arm, the thunderbolts itched
He regarded his servant sleeping there below,
He stretched to his fullest height, the lightning flashed,
The Great God Jupiter made his ultimate throw.

Fire   EARLY 303
aet. 59

"Fire! Fire! Look to the palace. It's burning."

"Stand back. Stand back. Let the city cohorts through.
They have the ladders and buckets to deal with the fire.
They can get the water from the city aqueduct.
We don't want the fire spreading to the rest of the city."

"What a night it's been, first the tremendous storm
And now this suspicious fire in the Imperial Palace."

"What do you think's the cause of this sudden fire?
The christians you say? I wouldn't be surprised.
It certainly looks as if they're striking back.
And what do you think? You have a knowing look.
Galerius' people you say? I don't see why.
Why would he want to burn his residence?
What's that? That is indeed ingenious.
You mean he's burnt the palace, so the Old Man
Will think it is the christians started the fire,
So he'll be even more determined to deal with them.
Either way the outlook for them looks thoroughly bleak!"

Listening to them talk was the Tribune Constantine,
Famous in later years for the useful knack
Of seeing signs in the heavens at appropriate times.
He it was that saw that night the thunderbolt.

The Senior Augustus Diocletian was furious,
Unceremoniously woken in the early hours,
Bundled out of bed while he was still half asleep,
Uneasy that he wasn't in control of all about him,
He feared that more than the fear of death itself.
This lack of order he would not tolerate,
He would regain control. It must be known
How this fire started in his private rooms.

DIOCLETIAN

The full process of law would immediately be applied
With thorough interrogation under torture,
Starting with the customary formal sacrifice
Which would incidently root out the christians.

The Senior Augustus was at work within the hour,
And felt better doing than thinking, for thought brought fear.
He presided over the questioning of his staff,
His personal servants, his eunuchs, each close to him.
He was determined that he would find out the cause
And obliterate this source of disrespect,
Both personal and more generally to the gods.

Now was the time for whips and red-hot brands,
Salt and vinegar rubbed into the wounds,
Slow burning according to the strict process of law.
They refused to tell of the origin of the fire,
Not from wilfulness but ignorance.
They refused to sacrifice, because they knew
They would earn their just reward in the life to come.
The man they worshipped had been scourged as well,
Salt and vinegar rubbed into his wounds,
From this they had learnt the habit of dying gladly.

The Council in Session   APRIL 303
aet. 59

The Council in session, the Senior Augustus alone,
The Caesar Galerius having precipitately withdrawn
On the occasion of a second fire at the Imperial Palace,
Saying to one and all he feared for his life;
The City of Nicomedia was infested with christians.

The business of the day is to consider reports from the East,
Trouble in Syria and at Melitene.
It is uncertain how far the christians were involved.
These were small affairs easily brought under control
But it is all too close for comfort to the Persian front.
Because of the second fire, which was quickly put out,
Everyone is anxious and on tenterhooks –
Not least the Senior Augustus sitting alone.

AGAINST THE CHRISTIANS

[From where I sit I can see it all!
How many times have I said that to myself?
But can I see it all? I thought so once,
With pride I thought I understood the way
All things pertaining to the Empire interlock.
I thought that applying pressure to a lever here
Would operate the delicate machine of state
To produce a result many thousand miles away.
The delicate machine I have made, consists of men –
Men who are fallible, men who act for themselves,
Men who conspire to deceive their masters and lords,
Men who follow false gods in spite of our laws,
How many such are here in the hall today?

When did I feel the machine getting out of control?
We tried to make the prices fair for all,
But every effort was distorted by men's greed,
The merchants suborned our servants and ignored our law,
Meanwhile these atheistic christians abound
Paying not the slightest respect to the ancient gods.
There was a time when I could put the machine to work,
When I could hold it all within my brain,
But now... What's that he says? I must attend.]

"These disturbances are not significant of themselves
But they are, My Lord, symptomatic of a general malaise
The longer these christians resist your authority
The greater will be the tendency for everyone
To disregard the authority of the state."

"Indeed. It is essential in the considered view
Of the Imperial Council, your Officers and your Friends,
That the christians are made to conform once and for all."

And so each of the counsellors had their say in turn,
And if the Senior Augustus had any doubts,
(Which I doubt if he did for by now he was fearful and angry)
The opinion of all in the council chamber confirmed
The necessity of the final act against the christians.

So a second edict was then drawn up and posted,
All bishops and other priests were to be arrested –
No need of confessions, their position was proof enough –

DIOCLETIAN

All members of the imperial household would sacrifice,
Starting with the Ladies Prisca and Valeria
So all, whatever their degree, would thereby show
Their loyalty to the Empire and to the Ancient Gods.

Valeria Speaks

"So it's come to this, that my loyalty has to be proved.
Does my Father doubt me that he demands I sacrifice
In front of everyone from the highest to the low?
I feel alone now that Galerius has gone,
Departed to Serdica to prepare for a new campaign.
I am well aware of the rumours which abound
Concerning my interest in the christian faith.
It's true that some of them were of help in Antioch.
I am glad that my nurse has not been faced with this,
The dear outspoken know-all, what would she have said?
But she cannot be disturbed, she is safe with her Christ.

I think too much of our Lords' deliberations
Have been concerned with the christians during the winter.
Much of the rest of the business of government
Has proceeded without either of them being involved
Wherever it can, but much has still been delayed.
My Father has grown old worrying about it all
And he and Galerius have been painfully estranged.
My pride is hurt that I'm asked to sacrifice
But I will do it gladly if it will give him strength
In his struggle to complete his task of restoration.

Now I must go seek my Mother and prepare
For the sacrifice which the imperial household shall make,
But how I wish all those familiar faces
Still were here among the household servants.
What a waste of so many useful reliable people."

Good News

Lucian and his fellow prisoners in Christ send greetings
To Cyril, Tyrannos and Dorotheus, brothers in Christ,
And to all the brethren in Antioch; be of good cheer.

AGAINST THE CHRISTIANS

The whole choir of martyrs jointly sends you greetings.
We bring you good news that Father Anthimus
Has met his end in the race of martyrdom.

Know you, that we in Nicomedia have seen
The glory of our Lord, this day, revealed to us
In the testimony of our brother Anthimus,
For he, with five of his council, have stood their ground
For Christ our Lord, and having been tempted, stood
For all to see as servants of the living God.

A new edict was proclaimed and many then were arrested,
The bishop, presbyters and the deacons, all,
Whether they had surrendered their books or not,
Then one by one they were called to sacrifice,
Starting with Anthimus as bishop of this town.

The Magistrate swore allegiance and sacrificed,
Sprinkling incense as you know is done
By custom and practice at the beginning of a trial,
And then called on Anthimus to sacrifice.
This the good man steadfastly refused to do.
"I have made my oath" said the Magistrate, "Now make yours".
Anthimus looked at him and quietly said:
"We are commanded never to take an oath.
It is written in sacred Scripture for all to see,
It is clear: 'Let your yes be yes and your no no'."
And each of the presbyters then were asked in turn,
And each refused as Anthimus had done;
So to the prison cell they were returned,
And on the following day brought back to court.

Anthimus, and the other five, were placed in the dock,
The Magistrate spoke: "Can you not now be sensible?"

He replied: "I am sensible and this is the way I live."

"Sacrifice to the gods," demanded the Magistrate.

"I will not because the sacred Scripture says:
'Whomsoever sacrifices to the gods
Save to the Lord alone, shall be destroyed'."

"Then, " said the Magistrate, "Sacrifice
To the Lord alone."

DIOCLETIAN

"That I will not do.
This is not the sort of sacrifice desired
By God, for in his sacred Scriptures it says:
'What to me is the multitude of your sacrifices?
I have had enough of the burnt offerings of goats and rams.'
The sacrifice which delights our God is the purest heart,
A sincere life, truth in speech and faith."

"Now sacrifice."

"I cannot. I never learnt how."

With that the judgement was made, the court was adjourned.
The Bishop and his five companions were led to the square.
The executioners stood there ready with sharpened swords.

Anthimus removed his garments, he made them a gift
For his executioner as is the age-old custom,
And then he turned and spoke for all to hear:

"I go to a perfect place where there are no aches,
No tired bodies, no slanders or arguments.
My dearest ones, pay heed to the commandments of God,
May the Lord bless you, watch over you, keep you safe.
Let us call upon the pure Almighty God
To whom is glory for ever and ever, Amen."

Each having spoken they all stretched out their hands,
The executioners' swords cut off their heads,
And so released at last their tireless souls.

Practical Economics SUMMER 303
aet. 59

"Move up the bench. Give us some elbow room.
You've been breathing down my neck for long enough."

"O.K. Mate. I'm glad to oblige I'm sure.
It wasn't by choice I was jammed up close to you.
Thanks be to the gods our visitors have been excused,
And most of them have shown good sense and gone.
I don't know what the world is coming to.
You cannot rely on anything any more.
There used to be a place for everything,
Everything in its place. You could count on it."

AGAINST THE CHRISTIANS

"That's true enough. Everyone had their place.
There was the Emperor on the top for all to see,
There were the generals and courtiers supporting him,
They had their soldiers and servants serving them,
And these had servants too which was just as well,
For these more humble folk would walk about
In ordinary places where you or I might be,
So we could perform the task the gods ordained
That the system remained in equilibrium."

"I haven't heard you speak like this for months.
The crowding must have really got you down;
It's a relief it's over now. We can relax.
But tell me why the system depends on us?"

"There must be movement if the system is to work.
The Emperor is rich, he has everything,
Of this he gives to his generals and courtiers much,
But not as much as they take without his leave.
How possibly can one man keep a watchful eye
On everything that there is, when he owns the world?
Now you know that soldiers are renowned as thieves,
And as for servants they're always on the take.
It is what is called 'the trickle down effect'.
A little of the Emperor's great and glorious wealth
Is carried in the pockets of these lesser serving men;
And that is precisely where you and I come in,
We pick those pockets as the ancient gods ordain;
The balance of the system is by us maintained."

"I knew that picking pockets is a noble trade,
But that it's a matter of economics is news to me.
I still don't see how we are essential to the system."

"What happens when we are caught and slung in here?
Either we are fined, or bribe our way out side,
Or perhaps our luck runs out and we are topped.
In that final case they take our clothes and goods.
Whatever happens the end result is the same.
Who gets the wealth which has trickled gradually down?
The prison officers, and tell me who they are?
They are the officers of the Emperor, it is him they serve.
So the system works, and that is thanks to us,

DIOCLETIAN

Redistribution agents of the Empire's wealth!"

"That makes me feel good, an essential cog in the wheel,
An agent of the Emperor. I feel justified.
More than can be said when we had all those others here.
I couldn't stand how they prayed and chanted psalms,
And the way they tried to turn us from our gods,
We who are agents of the Emperor."

"But the Emperor in his merciful wisdom acted
To relieve our suffering and set the place to rights.
He issued another edict, it is there on the door.
I am told it says, to mark the celebration
Of the twentieth year of his auspicious reign,
All christians are pardoned providing they sacrifice,
And that seems utterly reasonable to me."

"Laugh! I couldn't help but laugh to see
How many jumped at the chance to get outside,
And those that showed reluctance were forced to it.
The Emperor wanted everything in its place
With the prisons cleared for us, who are regulars."

"Only the stubbornest of christians are still inside.
They try the authorities' patience, that's a fact.
They are hard nuts to crack, but I must say I am impressed
With the habit the christians have of dying gladly."

THE TRIUMPH AND THE SHADOW
in which Diocletian celebrates his twenty years reign but to no avail

Getting Away

AD 303
aet. 59

They'd had enough of each other, all winter long
Cooped up in Nicomedia, Father and Son,
Arguing again and again what should be done
To contain the christians and to preserve the state.
They had become stale in their constant arguing,
Both were relieved to be on the move again,
Away from each other so each could now maintain
Their individual right to be Emperor.
Galerius departed first for Thessalonica,
Glad to be back on the campaign trail again,
The familiar struggle with the Carpi on the move,
Pushed up against the frontier by northern tribes.

The Senior Augustus now could concentrate
On the jubilee celebrations planned in Rome
To mark the opening of his twentieth year.
Now was the proper time to visit Rome,
Now that by all his labours, he had achieved
So much for the city which all would recognise,
It was right he should share his Triumph with Maximian
Giving thanks to the ancient gods in the City of Rome.

Summer was spent in the Danube provinces
Visiting places full of memories,
Durostorum in June, later in Sirmium.

DIOCLETIAN

Solace he sought in familiar sounds and scents,
Trying to recall the time when all seemed fair,
The object clear, with time enough to succeed.
Late in the year he came to the City of Rome
To celebrate and sacrifice to the gods.

The Triumph

ROME
20 NOVEMBER
AD 303
aet. 59

"Nineteen years to the day. Do they know this,
And do they care, the raucous Roman mob?
Here I stand in the chariot, gloriously robed,
Hardly room for the reinsman and the slave at my back,
He who by custom must murmur those warning words
Designed to remind me that I am an ordinary man.
The cheering mob see the slave holding the crown;
They cannot hear the words he quietly speaks
To deflect all ill from this place and from our self.

Nineteen years since the day I killed my boar;
Since that moment I had to move or all would be lost,
All that I'd striven for, for all those years.
Aper stood there in chains, looking at me.
He knew the way Numerian had met his death,
For that, he had to die that I might live
So I could serve the Empire in the way I have.
I raised my sword, a hush throughout the ranks,
We faced each other, all still, he dropped his eyes,
I drove the sword right in. There was a sigh,
Then the roar of the Army throbbing in my ears…
The roar of the people echoes here in Rome,
The uncomprehending response of ordinary men,
Excited by the triumph and all the gaudy show.

There in the other chariot is Maximian,
My brother and fellow worker in the noble quest,
Sharing the triumph and the cheers of the Roman mob.
Ahead the spoils of wars of the Tetrarchy,
Britain, the Rhine, victories on the Danube front,
Africa, and Egypt, and Persia greatest of all,
Each with its banner announcing least any forget
The place of the victories of Jove and of Hercules.

THE TRIUMPH AND THE SHADOW

Far ahead the Senators and the Magistrates process
Leading the way to the Temple of Capitoline Jove,
Where I, the Pontifex will sacrifice
In recognition of all that the gods have done
To preserve the realm and all who dwell therein.
Behind us march the men who fought the wars,
Legionaries drawn from each of the battle fronts
Proud of their part in making the Empire safe.

It is good to celebrate the twentieth year
Of our service to the state in this ancient way,
With customary pomp and traditional ceremony.
May all the people recognise the fact
That Jupiter rules and Diocletian serves the state."

Will He Stomach It? DECEMBER 303
aet. 60

"Well how do you think it's going, this visit of his?"

"The Triumph went well enough, which is just as well,
Considering all the preparatory work we have done.
The Senate determined the visit would be a success,
The first which the Senior Augustus has ever made
To Imperial Rome, the centre of the civilised world.
I shudder to think of the money we have spent, and the waste
If something happens to make the Senior Augustus displeased."

"But surely the statues we've placed in the forum show
The high regard in which we hold our lords,
And he will be pleased with the progress that has been made
In the construction of the new Baths. They are immense,
Overshadowing all the others as he well knew
When he approved the plans. He certainly builds to last."

"But there is in the man a puritanical streak,
You might almost call it meanness, I suppose.
You remember his reaction at the celebratory games,
How he disapproved of the excesses that he saw –
Not that the ordinary people thought it so,
When it comes to blood, they cannot have too much –
He declared the games were a religious happening,
In his presence as Censor moderation was required.

DIOCLETIAN

I fear the rowdy unruly Roman mob
Is not to the liking of our noble Lord."

"Let us hope his patience is not tried too much.
He plans to remain till the first of the coming year,
When he'll celebrate yet another consulship.
Meanwhile more feasts, celebrations and revelry,
Indeed I hope our Lord can stomach it."

The Final Straw

"I have had enough. That was the final straw,
The way the crowd behaved at the sacrifice,
Not only the common people but the senators.
They behaved as if they had seen it all before.
At the very moment of solemn dedication,
When the thoughts of everyone should concentrate
On the presence divine, and the meaning of the act –
I thank great Jove for support throughout my life,
I thank the gods of every place and clime,
That have enabled us to serve the state,
So Rome may last yet another thousand years.
And in the quiet I hear – there is no quiet,
Just murmuring chatter and lack of seriousness.

Processing on foot to the Capitol as is the custom,
The common people press in close on us,
So close the smelly breath and unkept teeth,
The great unwashed of Rome on holiday,
And as is custom I turn to greet them all
For I am first of equals here in Rome.
There in the crowd there is a familiar face,
I have seen him before but where I cannot recall,
He grins at me – and his grin turns to a jeer,
And his hand is making the sign of the hated cross,
And then I know where I have seen the man before –
In his other hand he holds a loaf of bread.

I have had enough of Rome. Why should I stay?
Why should I play to this crowd of ordinary men,
Who treat each day as another in Saturnalia?
Is it for this, the mob and the Roman effete,

THE TRIUMPH AND THE SHADOW

Who concern themselves with ancient precedence,
That I have striven exhaustedly for years?

But one more task remains that must be done,
However much I feel the uselessness
Of this charade of staying here in Rome.
I must convince Maximian how we'll complete
Our Imperial rule and peacefully transfer power
To our sons in the families of Jove and Hercules.
They each will choose their Caesars to follow them
And peacefully thus continue the imperial rule.

Before I take leave of Maximian, my brother and friend,
I must have his oath that when the time will come
He will retire as quietly as I shall do –
And after this time in Rome, I am ready to go,
But much remains which yet we have to do.
Almighty Jove, give me strength to finish my work."

Leaving Rome 20 DECEMBER 303
aet. 60

"God, it's cold – real brass monkey weather.
The driving rain and sleet – it is the end!
I thought I'd find advancement in his service,
But I think the ague is all that I will get.
There was I thoroughly enjoying my time in Rome,
Getting to know the ladies of the town –
I found they were impressed with all our titles,
And being a friendly type I must admit
I added a rank or two to impress them more –
When in comes my boss, who assists the Master of Office
And says we're off to Ravenna within the hour,
So here I am riding in the thick of the storm
To prepare the way for my boss, so he can prepare
The way for the Master of Office, so he can make sure
All is made ready for our lord the Senior Augustus.
High up here in the Apennines, all that I'll get,
By way of advancement, is strictly geographical, I fear."

Further down the Flaminian Way, closer to Rome,
A group of officials press on, in spite of the rain,
With their cloaks pulled closely to, they lower their heads,

DIOCLETIAN

Bending into the storm, they urge their horses on.
The Assistant to the Master of Office continues to worry;
He is new in the job so doesn't know what to expect,
And judging by his fellows' reactions, none of them do –
They've all been caught off guard by this change of plan,
The Emperor's sudden decision to quit the City.
"What's the Emperor think? It's simply done by magic,
The complicated task of moving court."

Among the close companions of the Emperor,
Escorting his litter as it leaves from the City of Rome,
The Master of Office rides slightly apart from the rest,
He is checking the details caused by this change of plan,
For although he has a staff to deal with all of this,
It rests on him that the Emperor's court runs smooth,
And his task is none the easier for these sudden whims.
He has served the Senior Augustus for some years now,
He has known him as a determined master, and one who plans,
Who sees connections not clear to other men,
Given to sudden moves as crises dictate –
"But where is the crisis which caused this sudden move?
It's an unhappy day when ordinary men have doubts,
And recognise their masters have doubts as well."

Inside the litter the Senior Augustus shivered,
The freezing wind found every seam and crack.
Around his shoulders, closer he pulled his cloak
He closed the shutter for he would be alone –
Alone with his thoughts, alone with his struggle in the world.
The cold wind blew, the driving rain and the sleet,
At every joint the Emperor's body ached,
His nerve ends raw – he felt completely alone.

Ravenna   January 304
aet. 60

However the Emperor feels, the work must go on.
Healthy or sick, the Empire has to be ruled.
To Ravenna the Roman Senators dutifully came
To invite Diocletian to be consul for the seventh time,
Which he humbly accepted. No reference was there made
To the change of scene or the precipitate flight from Rome.

THE TRIUMPH AND THE SHADOW

Despatches came to hand from Caesar Galerius.
The coming campaign season had to be planned;
The Carpi continue to trouble the Danube line,
The Senior Augustus agreed to handle this problem.
The barbarian tribes were on the move again
And other people were pushing the Carpi south.
They agreed they should solve this problem once and for all
By resettling the Carpi within the Imperial domain,
Having defeated them first thoroughly and brought them to heel.
Diocletian felt better discussing business like this,
Matters familiar which he confidently felt he could fix.

Then the vexed question of the christians was raised yet again –
Why couldn't Galerius have the sense to leave well alone?
But the Caesar was right, the problem of christians remained.
He could not dismiss the sight of the man in the crowd,
The jeering man with the loaf and the sign of the cross.
One final push was needed, they must conform,
So they prepared yet another edict and agreed it between them,
That every citizen in the Empire should sacrifice,
Proving their loyalty to the State for all to see.
Everyone should sacrifice without exception,
And for those who refused, the ultimate penalty — death.

Diocletian was exhausted when he finally made the decision,
Uneasy in mind, uncertain what the outcome might be.
He turned with relief to the business next in hand,
The report on his palace at Salona and how it progressed,
Just to think of this refreshed him, he could see the site,
He could smell the scent of the aspalathos growing there.
The building was progressing well according to the report,
But could he trust their word, he must go and see for himself.
There was time enough before the campaign began,
His Palace builders needed his advice.

Diocletian Visits His Palace

"My name is Zotikos, I am Master Mason,
Second only to the Master Builder on the site.
The Great Measure is held by him and him alone,
Without which the making of a building cannot proceed.

DIOCLETIAN

At the very beginning the rod is measured and cut,
And sacrifice is made to the god of the place,
Libations poured before the work can start
With all proportions ruled by the Master's rod.
But I digress, I was telling of the day he came,
Our patron, the owner, our client, the Emperor himself.

There we were standing, waiting by the Northern Gate,
The Master Builder and I and the heads of the guilds.
The third hour of the day was the time he was due to come,
When along the Salona road, to our surprise,
The councillors of the city, in disarray,
Came panting to a stop. 'Tell us we're just in time!
He isn't here, thank god,' or words like that.
Before we had had a chance of taking it in
Another group rode up, the Emperor's staff,
Not amused at looking rushed in front of us.
It appeared the Emperor had decided to cross by boat,
Much to the annoyance of those who were meant to plan
The careful considered progress of our Imperial Lord.

It was only much later that I learnt the reason why
The Emperor had decided to approach the palace by boat –
I learnt it from the very highest possible source,
But that is a story I will tell you another time –
When he was a boy in Salona he would sometimes go
To this wild place with others from his school,
Collecting berries, fishing, playing about,
As boys will do. Then there was no road,
They reached the headland across the bay by boat.
I heard from someone else how he got the land:
One of the very first things he did as Emperor
Was to find who owned the headland across the bay,
And when the owner learnt who admired his land,
He was pleased to make a gift of it to him!

One of the Emperor's staff sorted us out,
Lined us up so we were ready to greet out Lord,
The Council, the Imperial Staff, and then ourselves,
We who had worked on his palace for four long years.
He came in a litter borne from the shore of the bay,
Escorted only by his personal bodyguard.

THE TRIUMPH AND THE SHADOW

He looked much older than he had in Antioch,
When I saw him sacrificing with Galerius.
But he looked refreshed and eager when he saw the gate –
It looked good with the open arch above the lintel,
The spaces ready for statues, handsome indeed,
Similar to work we had done in Antioch.

The formal greetings done, the libations made,
The Emperor would see his palace, each tile and stone.
He insisted the Master Builder escorted him
Together with a few of us who had done the work.
In earnest then the inquisition began,
'Why was the stone different in the Northern Gate?
How would it weather? And what of the remaining stone?
From where came the tiles, and what was their quality?
Had the sphinxes yet come from Egypt, and the columns too?
Were we clear where they had to be put? Let us now go and see.'
The more questions he asked, the younger he seemed to become,
The more exhausted we felt, but exhilarated nevertheless,
For here was a patron worth building palaces for.

I remember the way he reacted when he first went in
And saw the courtyard outside his residence,
Four pillars of crimson granite and the pediment
Over the entrance with arcading on either side,
He glowed with pleasure as if he had made it himself,
And the view from his private quarters to the open sea –
The sun broke through, the gods were kind to us.

Then our problems started – we had been too fortunate.
The Emperor wished to stay within the palace
In spite of it being in such an unfinished state.
We all had thought he would use the basileia,
Maintained in Salona especially for such occasions.
Within a matter of days some rooms were ready,
But most of his staff were quartered in Salona town,
And none of this made the building work any easier.

There then was the business of the christians which made things worse
There were many of us who had come from Antioch,
Where we had worked on the palace that he'd had built
In the middle of the Orontes on the site of Valerian's fort.

DIOCLETIAN

Many were christians, for Antioch was full of them,
And they had established a church among the workers
With one called Domnius as bishop to tend for them.

That was bad enough, then the fourth edict was posted,
That was shortly before the Emperor himself arrived.
Everyone had to sacrifice without exception.
We got the necessary certificates before he came,
To avoid any trouble arising while the Emperor was here.
But then some enthusiasts among the workers began
To speak of the christian god to the Emperor's men.
Four of the bodyguard then refused the test,
Proclaiming their faith in the christ and asked for death.
I worried then that the building would be delayed.
Why couldn't they concentrate on the work in hand?

So the Emperor's visit which started so promisingly
Ended abruptly with his departure back to the north,
But not before the recalcitrant bodyguards
And Domnius the cause of the trouble, were executed,
An added attraction to the games the council put on
To honour the visit to Salona of the Senior Augustus.

So we can return to the business of building once more.
There is still much to do, but I will never forget
The look in the Emperor's eye when he first saw his palace.
I expect he will be back soon enough to see it again."

REDUCED TO THIS
in which Diocletian decides it is time
for younger men to carry the burden

Nightmare   SUMMER 304
aet. 60

"That summer was a nightmare, a summer I will never forget.
The Emperor was restless, always changing his mind.
If he changed it once, he changed it a hundred times,
And I was responsible for planning his itinerary.
I worked with the Praetorian Prefect and Master of Office.
In normal times they left me completely alone
And only when sudden changes upset their plans,
Did they interfere, start breathing down my neck,
And worrying which of them I reported to.

I should have guessed that we'd have problems when we left Rome;
This we did without notice, purely on the Emperor's whim.
We managed somehow to arrange for things in Ravenna
And then he suddenly decided to visit Salona –
He wished to see his new palace which was being built –
And that is not an easy route to plan at all.

Salona had its problems, but we managed to have them solved.
He wished to stay in the palace and not in the town.
All seemed set fair – he played the architect,
But then he must move again, and that at once,
Troubled by christians in his bodyguard.
He had them put to the sword in the amphitheatre,
Then we were off again to the frontier in the north.
For in spite of all our troubles we had a campaign to fight.

DIOCLETIAN

These sudden moves did the Emperor no good at all.
He was ill when he came to Ravenna, he didn't improve.
The Emperor travelled in a litter wherever he went,
The few times he felt better there was action everywhere.
It was as if he sensed there was no time remaining
For all that the Gods required of him to do;
And every day he seemed to waste away."

In a Box

PANNONIA
SUMMER 304
aet. 60

My world reduced to this –
Carried confined in a box –
Left   right   left –
Half of it's filled with my flesh –
Itching carcass and rot –
Left   right   left –
The air which my body leaves –
Within my box, it smells –
Left   right   left.

The gentler ones carrying now –
Easing my body's sores –
Left   right   left –
That's what it's comes to at last –
Paying homage with care of their hands –
Left   right   left –
And I, the Senior Augustus –
Pathetically grateful for this –
Left   right   left.

Is this how Numerian felt? –
And he no more than a boy –
Left   right   left –
But Numerian had to go –
The dust got into his eyes –
Left   right   left –
And now it's my eyes that itch –
Alone in my world of a box –
Left   right   left.

I must have slept. Great Jupiter – it smells.
Let us see where we are. That's better – the morning breeze –

REDUCED TO THIS

The bearers still carry their load – hour on, hour off –
There is a rest house at the foot of the hill. There we must stop.
For there's still much to do – and so little time.
How long have I been cooped up here in this box?

Return to Nicomedia   28 AUGUST 304
aet. 60

No fanfare for the Emperor in Nicomedia,
The litter reached the Palace late at night.
The word soon spread to all whatever degree,
Their Lord and Master Diocletian was close to death.
Many there were who had served no other master,
The very foundations of their lives seemed to them threatened.

The Palace staff tiptoed nervously about their work,
No unnecessary words, quietness throughout.
It was as if they feared the slightest sound
Would upset the delicate balance of their world,
By finally putting the Emperor's life at risk,
Launching their Master on the ultimate voyage.

Some there were who counted on his strength of will.
All knew the plan to dedicate the circus
To mark the twentieth year of the Emperor's reign.
He was determined to be present at the ceremonies,
He would not allow death to intervene.
At least the Palace staff could rest till then.

The great day came, the city in festive mood,
The Emperor struggled stubbornly to fulfil his part,
But the state of their Lord was evident to all.
Here was a man on the very brink of death.
The day which dawned in hope ended in despair,
They felt they were witnessing a rite of passage.

The Emperor was hidden within an inner room
Tended by his body servants and doctors alone,
But all was known, they listened to every breath.
Throughout the Palace and the City everywhere,
They waited with solemn prayer and sacrifice.
This was the man necessary for the State.

At the shortest day of the year his breathing stopped

DIOCLETIAN

In the deepest coma. The doctors held their breath,
The Palace servants wept – all seemed lost.
For one whole night it was thought that he was gone,
Then in the earliest hours the merest murmur
Proved that the Emperor had pulled back from the brink.

There he remained on the edge for three long months,
Rumours ran riot, he kept to the inner room.
And then with hope nearly gone, as the days lengthened,
The Emperor presented himself to his court again,
But what a change there was, for he had aged,
He looked as if he had seen the face of death.

Diocletian Decides

MARCH 305
aet. 61

The frustrated god hardly knew what to do.
Only through humans can gods themselves maintain
By having living people believe in them;
If only the dead believe, the gods shall wane.

Jupiter looked at the world, he almost despaired.
Everywhere fewer worshipped the Olympians.
From out the East new mysteries prevailed
With life after death and forgiveness of all sins.

Now his servant had been on the brink of death,
A wiser man but less committed too.
What Jupiter needed was a man of utter faith
Who believed in him completely through and through.

— ✳ —

The Caesar Galerius was coming to court at last,
All winter long they had expected him.
With the Emperor ill they needed Galerius.
At the pinnacle of imperial power there was a void,
No decisions made, the Empire seemed to drift,
While Galerius considered the future and bided his time.

Now with the Emperor recovered, Galerius moved.
He was clear his time had come at last to succeed;
For thirteen years he had fought the Empire's wars,
Continuously on campaign risking his life,

REDUCED TO THIS

While others celebrated the victories,
But failed to win the war for peoples' minds.
The ancient gods received little respect,
The christians must be dealt with once and for all,
The ancient verities must still prevail,
People must believe completely through and through.

Diocletian looked forward to seeing Galerius,
For he was a son to him not only in name,
But in spirit too for they had served the state,
They had strived together, much had been achieved.
He still could see Galerius of the streaming locks
Riding helter-skelter through the storm.
As old men will do he remembered what he would:
Galerius smiling with his daughter in Sirmium;
Galerius and he celebrating in Antioch
Before the new Palace entrance at the end of the war;
Forgotten completely Galerius standing alone
In the heat of the sun returning his stern regard.
He thought of Galerius younger than he really was
And forgot what he had done by that same age.

So Galerius came and greeted the Senior Augustus
He wished him well, his health now being recovered,
Then turned to business briskly without further ado:
"Your sickness this winter has made it clear to all
How essential to the efficient government of the State
The presence is of a firm and active ruler.
You have done so much for the State in your twenty years
But the time has surely come to rest and relax."

Now Diocletian had had these very thoughts himself
But to have them spoken by another threatened him.
It is one thing to think an act however extreme,
But put in words the thoughts grow closer to fact.
Both men knew for long there had been a plan
That each Augustus would in due course retire;
The Caesars would succeed and each choose Caesars too.

Now Galerius was saying that 'in due course' was now,
While the older man thought there was still much to do
Which he had the necessary experience to undertake.

DIOCLETIAN

— ✽ —

No sleep for Diocletian, his brain raced on,
Thoughts tumbled one on another, ill disciplined:
The tortoise crossing the road, the peasant by the Nile,
The silence in the wood as the boar waited to charge,
The sand on the sea shore in Gaul as the tide flowed in,
Day in, day out, time is eaten up.
No time left to consider how to act,
Time to decide with what wisdom there is to hand,
The accumulated wisdom of one man Diocletian,
But all he felt was exhaustion and jumbled thoughts.

Then in that land between sleep and wide awake
He knew. Everyday the tide would ebb and flow,
The sand would shift, each grain would change its place,
And then lie smooth as far as the eye could see.
The time had come for others to bear the load.

— ✽ —

"I have decided the time has come to implement
The long standing plan we have had for the continuance
Of our imperial policies for the Empire's good.
To that effect it is my pleasure and intent
To withdraw from the daily toil of government.

[It is done. No going back. We have moved on.
Galerius has grown in power as I speak the words,
And I, Diocletian, grow less.]

I will resign my authority and retire
To Salona, to my palace newly built.
My brother Maximian will at the same time retire,
He has sworn that he will comply when the time will come.
You Galerius, and Constantius in the West,
Will assume the august authority and power."

This was acknowledged somewhat brusquely, Diocletian thought.
Then they turned to decide who the new Caesars should be
And Diocletian learnt how quickly power had shifted.

Diocletian spoke: "The Caesars should be appointed
By common agreement among the four of us."

REDUCED TO THIS

"What need is there of agreement of the other two?
They must accept whatever we decide."

"Fortunately that is no problem. They will agree
Since we must plainly appoint their two sons.
Maxentius, Maximian's son is linked to you
By having been given your daughter's hand in marriage.
That Maxentius would one day be appointed Caesar
We had firmly in mind when we made the match.
Constantine has been with us here in the East,
Serving at different times with both of us.
We both have found him worthy of higher things."

"It is essential we appoint those with whom I can work."

"That I agree, Galerius, but why not these men?"

"Maxentius is certainly not worthy, he shows no respect
Neither to me nor his father, he is utterly full of contempt.
If as a private citizen he behaves like this
How he would behave as a Caesar is frightening to think."

"But Constantine is popular with the citizens and the Army too.
He shows promise and I believe that when he will rule,
He will be judged even better and more merciful
Than his father Constantius, and he has ruled well."

"But in that case I will not be able to have a free hand…

[That is the point! But why not? He has to rule.
I chose my Caesars and I did what I wished –
But I convinced my colleagues. I used no force.]

…I must be able to control the Caesars whom we appoint.
There's so much to do."

                    "Whom have you in mind?"

"Severus."

        "What! That drunken devotee of the dance?
He who treats the night as day!"

                    "The same.
He deserves it. He has been loyal as an army commander.

DIOCLETIAN

He is acceptable to Maximian. That I have made sure.
I discussed this with him when we met during the winter."

[So that was what you were doing when you were needed here.
You have planned carefully indeed, Galerius, for this meeting.]

"Whom do you propose as Caesar in the East?"

"This man here. He's my nephew, Maximin Daia."

"But he has no experience. He's only just a Tribune.
Why yesterday he was a ranker in the Guards
And only came to court a year ago."

"I can rely on these men. I know them. I've tested them."

"So be it then. The Empire will be in your hands.
You must make a success of these men whom you have chosen.
I have laboured long and watched carefully over the state.
It has come to no harm, and now it is up to you."

The Last Parade

NICOMEDIA
1 MAY 305
aet. 61

Now see again the plain outside the city,
The place that witnessed twenty years before
The proclamation of Diocles as Emperor.
See now on rising ground a monument,
Jupiter raised on a column marks the spot.
Again contingents from all the legions stand,
Ready to take their part in the ceremony,
Essential to the proper making of Emperors.

"I don't like it. I don't like it at all.
All this change I find extremely unsettling.
The Old Man's been Emperor for as long as we have served,
He knows the ropes and besides he looks the part."

"Oh. I don't know. Change is not so bad.
Think of the money we'll get when this is done.
Our fathers still talk of the money they received
When they were here twenty years ago."

"Silence in the ranks! The Emperor is about to speak."

And so it was that the Emperor Diocletian

REDUCED TO THIS

Addressed his people for the final time.
He rose to speak. What could he say to them,
To make them understand what they should do
To better live their lives in this fearsome world,
What could he say that they would understand
The problems the Empire had faced, the obstacles,
Which had been overcome during his reign,
What of the threats and difficulties to come,
Some clearly seen and many yet unknown?

He could speak of stability, he had reigned for twenty years,
Now he planned to do what no one else had done.
He would retire, surrender his authority,
Peacefully pass the imperial power to another.
In this he had succeeded – he had survived.

He could speak of the barbarians kept without the gate
No longer running wild throughout the land,
Trade flowing free, the highways well maintained,
He could speak of peace and the countryside well tilled.
He looked at the faces of the soldiers, massed below,
He saw the citizens, the courtiers and the common people,
And he thought he saw the man with the loaf of bread.

Could they comprehend what a struggle this work had been?
The limits of one man's strength, the inadequacy,
The exhaustion borne of will-power constantly used,
And lasting illness unto the brink of death.

And then, he spoke simply – not of these things,
But rather that he was ready now to go;
He was tired, seeking to rest after his work.
He was handing over the imperial power at last
To younger men more able to carry the load,
And was appointing other Caesars to take their place.

Immediately murmurs of interest throughout the crowd,
Their speculation would now be satisfied.
(All knew that Galerius and Constantius
Would now succeed as Augusti in East and West,
But the question was – who would the Caesars be?)
Then they were named, first Valerius Severus
To be Caesar to Constantius Augustus in the West,
And here – here they expected Constantine,

DIOCLETIAN

He was standing among the officers in the entourage –
And here the Caesar to serve with Galerius
Will be Maximin Daia.

                        "Who is that? Is it someone new?"

"Has Constantine changed his name? It is common practice."

Then Galerius pulled young Daia from the back,
Pushed him towards the old man, so all could see.
They realised indeed this Caesar was completely new.

Then the Senior Augustus removed his purple cloak,
Draped it on the young man's shoulders and left the stage.
A covered chariot was waiting, there was no delay.
Diocles was driven directly through the city.

Silence in the ranks, no word from the citizens,
Surprised by the choice of the unknown man as Caesar,
Stunned by the suddenness of the great Diocletian's departure,
Their Emperor who had ruled them for more than twenty years,
Solving problems which had troubled the Empire for many centuries,
With a toughness of mind and ability to have new thoughts.

This he now showed in the way he abdicated.
It was not done; it never had been done,
But now he did it, removing his purple cloak,
Just like that – he became Diocles again.

THE LAST CHAPTER
in which Diocles is completely alone
and the Almighty God moves in a mysterious way

A Quiet Life by the Sea

S<small>ALONA</small>
A<small>D</small> 305
aet. 61

"And how do I like it here? It is certainly quieter!
When we were in Nicomedia, it was all go.
Couriers arriving at all hours, day and night.
Now we feel rushed if there is more than one a week.
But my job as Chamberlain to the retired Augustus
Is less stressful without a doubt than the one before.
Then I was Head of the Bedchamber, I had held the post
During all the time the Emperor Diocletian was sick.

I had succeeded the worthy Dorotheus in the job,
He it was, you know, who suffered for his faith,
He was a christian and refused to sacrifice.
That was a terrible time, you could smell the fear,
There were many of the domestic staff who met their death,
Summarily strung up, then bundled into sacks,
Weighted with stones and thrown into the open sea.
Not all of us eunuchs were christians, whatever was said,
(But we all have a weakness for gossiping I can hear you say)
So I remained and succeeded Dorotheus in the Emperor's service.

Here at the new palace by Salona we still observe
The daily routines of court though there are few of us.
There is still the Salutio at the beginning of the day;
The Pater Augusti, for that is his title now,
Or plain Diocles which he sometimes seems to prefer,

DIOCLETIAN

Presents himself and he is greeted by whoever is there.
I could weep when I think of the hundreds that used to come,
The many more kept away, not allowed to approach,
But it does not seem to worry my Master at all.
He returns our greetings with utmost courtesy.
It is only when there is a new face that it shows,
That he is aware how much his world has changed.
His eyes light up, he concentrates his gaze,
He questions the newcomer in detail about his affairs.
He is like a fasting man glimpsing a feast.

His day is full but not with affairs of state.
He discusses progress on the building, it never stops.
He knows the character of every stone and tile,
Each elevation, perspective and plan, by heart.
Zotikos grows old patiently listening to him,
Planning minor changes to the grand design.

Then there is the garden within the palace grounds,
This is something new he has found since coming here,
Spyros, the Master Gardener, is good at his job
Which is just as well for the plants in the palace garden
Have to conform as good citizens did in the past –
At least, that is how my Lord remembers it,
For being retired my Master recalls with care
Only those things which complete his picture of life."

The Garden   AD 305
aet. 61

"Gardens don't grow in a day, but we must do our best
To make the palace look settled, not raw and new.

I was not here when the Senior Augustus came
To inspect, last year, the progress which had been made.
Building work and the making of gardens, they do not mix,
The workmen constantly trampled over the beds,
Anyway the Master Builder changed his mind,
Putting a building just where I had planned for flowers,
So I was away buying cyprus and other young trees,
And arranging for hedges of box to be prepared
For transplanting as soon as the building was complete.

Imagine then my dismay when I returned
To hear from Zotikos that he believed
The Emperor would take up residence in a very short time.
He said for sure it was just a hunch he had,
But I had experience of Zotikos's hunches.
I wasn't going to risk delaying the start any longer.
One good thing was the layout had now been agreed,
So at least I knew exactly where I had to work.
In addition to the courtyards within the private quarters,
There was to be a colonnaded garden
To the right of the street as you enter the Northern Gate –
Just like that – not any consultation at all!
It was as well I had planned and had my plants prepared.

We worked hard that summer and luckily it was not too hot.
We brought in good earth, disposed of the builders' rubble,
We made libations and prayed that the winter be mild.
We bought in box hedges, they were really too old to transplant,
We prayed – how we prayed – that the overlarge plants would take.
Cyprus we had, some in pots, with laurel and myrtle,
Oleander, acanthus, viburnum, small specimens still,
But carefully placed for their appearance when fully grown.
Ivy and vines which would grow to give summer shade,
Poppies and lillies for colour and numerous roses.

The gods were kind – the spring was exceptionally mild
So when we heard the news that Emperor had retired –
Zotikos's hunch had proved correct again –
That he would be arriving within the next few days,
The garden was ready, just – but nonetheless there
Making the palace appear a welcoming place.

What is a home without a garden, I ask?"

— ⁕ —

"After all our work I was pleased the Emperor noticed.
On the morning after his arrival I was in the garden,
Supervising the workers, who were thinning out the poppies.
There were so many, they threatened to spoil the effect
I was trying to achieve close to the Northern Gate.
He was not as tall as I thought he would be,
Formally dressed, but simply, he came alone –
A private citizen on holiday.

DIOCLETIAN

I remember he asked me what the men were doing
And that led us on to discussing garden design,
How a garden should be an extension of the building plan,
Embellish the structure and provide additional space
For comfort and recreation in the open air.

And I remember he said a garden must be useful too,
I caught a glimpse of the Emperor that he had been,
I told him gardens were capable of producing food!
We could incorporate cabbages among the flowers –
And so we did, and that was what interested him.

He used to come to the garden whenever he could
If there was no pressing business he would come and work –
No toga then, just tunic and broad brimmed hat –
I showed him what to do and gradually he learnt,
How to sow, then how to thin out and then transplant,
How to use a line to make sure the row is straight,
How to ensure the cabbage is watered but not too much.

And that is how I taught an Emperor
How to become close to being a god,
How to enable living things to grow."

The Deluge

AD 305–308
aet. 61–64

Diocletian was a wily lord.
He was essential to the state.
This was proved when he withdrew
And left the others to their fate.

Severus was Caesar in the West
In support of Augustus Constantius,
But the city of Rome was being held
By Maximian's son, Maxentius.

Now Constantius' son Constantine
Was at the court of Galerius,
Who refused Constantius' request,
"Please send our dearest son to us."

THE LAST CHAPTER

Galerius then changed his mind,
Constantine was allowed to go.
He joined his father who was sick –
A fact Galerius did not know.

Constantius died in the city of York,
His army proclaimed Constantine,
Alarming Galerius for Constantine then
Held all to the west of the Alpine line.

Galerius accepted him as Caesar
With Severus Augustus in the West.
Constantine agreed that he might be
Of legal title clearly possessed.

But Maxentius called himself Augustus
Sitting safely there in Rome,
Popular with the citizens,
He treated the city just like home.

Then Maxentius decided he needed help.
So persuaded his father out of retirement,
Thus Maximian became Augustus again
By accepting the purple his son had sent.

Now Severus marched on the city of Rome
But Maximian and his son were safe inside.
His army mutinied, Severus retired,
In Ravenna he was forced to suicide.

Maximian allied with Constantine
Named him Augustus like his son,
Married him to his daughter Fausta,
And so the whole of the West was one.

This was something Galerius
Could not tolerate at all.
Therefore he invaded Italy,
But was also held outside Rome's wall.

Galerius beat a hasty retreat.
This success went to Maximian's head.
He tried to depose Maxentius;
He failed therefore to Gaul he fled.

DIOCLETIAN

Constantine received his father-in-law,
But kept him and the army far apart,
For Maximian was devious in his old age,
But Constantine proved just as smart.

Galerius did not like what he saw,
Three Augusti in the West.
He lacked the authority to put things straight.
He didn't know what to do for the best.

Diocletian had been retired three years,
See in that time what had come to pass.
Galerius decided to call on him
To help him solve this terrible farce.

The Old Warhorse Smells The Smoke

SALONA
AD 308
aet. 64

"They think that I am deaf in my old age –
But I could hear what they said – every single word!
Something about my looking pleased with myself,
About an old warhorse excited by the battle smoke.
Well why not? It's not everyone who retires
And is asked to return to help sort out the mess –
A mess, what is more, created by those younger men,
The ones who so recently wanted me out of the way.
I wouldn't be human if I wasn't a little bit flattered,
And excited at the prospect of real life problems again.

I went to the garden later than usual that day
Because we had a courier from Galerius,
And the man must needs be questioned by me myself.
He had come direct so had the news at court.
He could give those extra bits of information,
Essential to understanding the politics
Behind the formal words of the despatch.

From the words and the interrogation it is clear
That Galerius thinks the situation grim,
Even more fragile than had appeared to us,
From what we had gathered here in our seaside retreat.
The nub of the problem is my brother Maximian.
He listened to me but not to these younger men.

THE LAST CHAPTER

Power is his life, he was loath to surrender it,
And given half a chance by his son, he is back in the game;
But both of them are illegal; the law must prevail.

Constantine at least has maintained his legality –
By the skin of his teeth – but Galerius recognised him.
He let him go, by the gods that is a tremendous tale,
The way the young man seized his chance and rode,
Hamstringing the remounts at every posting house,
All the way to his father on the coast of furthest Gaul,
And when Galerius woke and found him gone –
His permission given informally at the dinner hour –
His utter fury was equalled only, I am told,
When he found that none could follow for the horses were lame.

(I admired the young man for that, but I must admit,
I'd a twinge of conscience for perhaps I'd let him down.
He had looked on me as a mentor but I didn't respond.
I'd assumed he'd succeed as Caesar – he must have known –
But when the time came to retire I didn't insist –
My god, I was tired – but the fact remains I failed,
Failed to ensure he'd succeed to the place he deserved.)

His father died as you know, and young Constantine
Was proclaimed Augustus by his father's men.
I remember thinking that this was a man who'd go far
When I heard how he handled Galerius afterwards.
He accepted the junior title of Caesar. He'd wait.
He had the reality of power in the West. He had time –
He seemed to know he was destined for ultimate power,
Just as I had been when I sought the fated boar.
But Galerius seems more concerned with Maxentius,
Usurping the name of Augustus, safe in Rome,
And his father who won't retire, disturbing the peace.
It is with my former messmate Maximian,
That Galerius wants my help, for that I am called.
Doubtless he has other plans for which he wants
The public support of the former Senior Augustus.

I'd suspected that something like this was likely to happen
Ever since my name was proposed as consul again –
This is my year and I must earn my keep! –

DIOCLETIAN

It is significant as well that my daughter Valeria
Has been honoured with the title Augusta. Yes, I am pleased –
But I think I understand just what all this means,
Galerius has need of me – and I am pleased.

If I am deaf, then I am selectively deaf,
I am certain I heard what Spyros the Gardener said:
'I am sorry he is going back to politics.
He's the makings of a gardener if only he'd concentrate'."

Diocletian is Tempted

CARNUNTUM
AD 308
aet. 64

Carnuntum in November, the cold wind blows,
The frontier troops in the watchtowers look to the north,
The tribesmen tend their herds and all is quiet.
The defences carefully built over twenty years,
They still hold firm in spite of discord within.

"That much I did achieve in all those years
Of striving to save the Empire from falling apart.
I hope they appreciate that, now that I have gone,
All the hopes we had, the schemes, the policies,
Have come to this, a world made safe and sound
That ambitious men may struggle in civil war."

The three men met, survivors of the noble quest,
The quest Diocletian led to save the realm.
Galerius, who in three brief years had seen
The second tetrarchy disintegrate –
He had tried to continue what Diocletian began
But death and disloyalty had intervened,
And now he needed that authority which he lacked
To establish the legal framework once again.

Maximian came, excited by the power
Which he had retaken in spite of his sacred oath,
Apprehensive what his brother in arms would say,
But nonetheless proud that there was still a part for him.

And the old man came and he certainly felt his years,
He tired more quickly, he lacked the exercise

THE LAST CHAPTER

Of regular daily business of the affairs of state.
He had lost the art of dealing with diversity;
He could only concentrate on one thing at a time,
But he was determined the rule of law should prevail,
And his plan for the imperial succession be made to work.
After many days of discussion, the decisions were made
With all the authority of the former Senior Augustus:

* Maximian was to retire a second time;

* Constantine was recognised as Caesar again,
  For Maximian had not the right to name him Augustus;

* Maxentius was branded an enemy of the people;

* Licinius, a companion of Galerius for many years,
  Was invested as Augustus with authority to rule in the West;

* Galerius would continue as Augustus in the East,

* Maximin Daia would remain as Caesar there.

(All that now remained that had to be put in hand
Were the actions necessary to make these decisions, fact.)

But it need not have ended like this, it nearly didn't.
One evening early in the conference, all three were there.
Galerius was tired, exhausted by the constant strain
Of exercising the authority of goverment.
Maximian was speaking, eagerly holding forth:
"Things aren't what they used to be – no rule of law.
When you and I…"

                        ["no rule of law?" – what nerve!
Here am I, Galerius, spending all my time
Trying to exert the imperial rule of law,
While this wild man defies authority.
And what of the other old man, what does he think,
Sitting in the candlelight, listening, his eyes half closed.]

["You and I" – indeed, you and I have done so much –
That early morning when we saw the dromedaries
Fleeing with Zenobia and then the hectic chase,
The old witch in Tungria who foretold the boar,
The killing of the boar itself, you stood by me,
You loyally served as my very Hercules.]

DIOCLETIAN

"...We worked so well together Diocles –
Calling you that doesn't come easily,
Why can't we call you Diocletian once again?
Why don't you come again, we need you now,
The three of us could quickly put things right.
Return again and save us, Diocletian.
You are a man necessary to the state."

His words hung on the air. The candle flickered.
Galerius looked at the two and held his breath,
Half of him wanted the old man to say he would,
He felt so alone in his struggle to rule the world.
Maximian watched and waited. There was a draught.

Diocletian was tempted – but in that moment he knew it.
He felt the excitement drumming through his brain
The excitement of dealing with important matters of state
And he felt the fear of having to make up his mind –
Each drop of fear gradually reducing his strength,
And he felt the warmth of the earth in the new dug plot.
He looked at the two men watching waiting for him.

"Maximian, If you knew the pleasure my cabbages give..."

"Cabbages? [Has he gone mad?]"

"Yes, Cabbages I say.
If you knew the joy I get from planting them –
Sowing the seeds, seeing them multiply,
Thinning them out so they grow healthily –
If you could see the cabbages that I have planted
In my garden at the palace at Salona with my own hands,
You would not suggest I give up the pleasure that brings
For the pursuit of power. That is for younger men."

Galerius relaxed. The moment of decision had passed.

No Solace SALONA
EARLY 309
"The old man came back, so I have extra help; *aet.* 65
But I lost my bet, I had wagered he would never return.
I was certain the lure of politics would prevail.
Now the spring has come and the days lengthen again,

THE LAST CHAPTER

We see more of him for he comes every day,
But he is getting older, he just stops and stares,
Standing and looking about with unfocussed eyes.
Meanwhile we get on with our work, the weather is good,
It is the growing-time in the garden. There is much to do."

— * —

I am here. What use is that to me or anyone?
Even the gardeners go about their work
Whether I am here or not. They don't need me.
I said the cabbages gave me joy. I lied.
I really thought I meant it at the conference;
Maximian believed me but now I do not know.
I who ruled the world reduced to this,
Training cabbages to keep in line.

— * —

"Zotikos, we have got to finish the mausoleum.
We still need a decision about the decorative frieze.
Everything else is done but that remains.
I would be shamed if the time came and it wasn't complete.
Every day I see him it worries me more and more –
The frieze I mean, we really need a decision."

"I'll try. I'll try. But he will not pay attention –
He stares into the distance. I don't know what he sees.
Then he turns and nods and murmurs 'Tomorrow. Tomorrow.'
But it shall be done! I will tackle him as soon as I can,
For we owe it to ourselves that his final resting place
Is meet and suitable for a man who ruled the world."

— * —

Why can't they leave me alone? I wish they would.
Questions, always questions. But what is the use?
What does it matter how they fix the frieze?
The cold wind will blow however well they build.
But we won't be here to feel it, or admire the frieze.
We will have gone, left nothing, not a thing.

DIOCLETIAN

A Dying Lord

SALONA
AD 311
aet. 67

"I am concerned about my master, I say it myself.
It is hard to be the chamberlain to a dying Lord.
I love the man, and it hurts me to see him die.
When he returned from Carnuntum I sensed relief,
He would not have to involve himself in life,
But as time went by I think he felt deprived.
He spent many brooding hours, he would not attend
To the regular business of living an ordinary life.

It was clear to us the decisions made at Carnuntum
Depended on the agreement of those who were not there.
Those of us who had known the Tribune Constantine
Doubted that he would accept demotion again.

Why should he agree to be Caesar when he'd been Augustus,
Just to fit neatly into a plan of succession.
So it proved, and Daia in the East objected as well.
Galerius tried to maintain the Carnuntum agreement,
But after a while we ended with no fewer than six,
Six Augusti uneasily watching each other.

None of us believed Maximian would really retire,
Though he agreed to that at Carnuntum in front of my Lord,
So it wasn't a surprise to hear he'd tried to usurp
Constantine's power in Gaul, but Maximian failed.
I remember my Lord hearing Maximian was dead,
No real sense of loss – just emptiness.
It was as if they had both died already.

Then early in the following year our World collapsed.
It was in the spring we heard Galerius was ill,
And almost at once we heard that he was dead,
Struck down by a foul disease, he was full of decay,
His great body rotted, the smell was everywhere.
In his final days he issued an edict allowing
Everyone to worship as they would, so all are free
The worshippers of the ancient gods, the christians,
All of whatever faith that they may pray
For the wellbeing of the Empire and the Emperor.

And how does he take it? Not well. He now is the last,
The others with whom he ruled the world are gone.

I am not sure what he feels about the final edict.
Certainly Galerius had been at least as fierce
In attacking the christians, and in the end he had failed.
I know that my Lord after receiving the news,
Spends even more time, standing on the southern wall,
Looking out to sea, saying nothing, watching the waves."

Constantine's Time Has Come

ARLES
LATE 311
aet. 67

The City of Arles in Gaul, the world is alive
With the bustle of eager men preparing to march.
The Augustus Constantine is going to war
Against the vile Maxentius waiting in Rome.

Adding insult to injury, Maxentius proclaims to the world
His father, Maximian, was a god who had been forced to die,
Besieged alone by the ungrateful Constantine.

The furious Constantine, in turn, condemns
The memory of Maximian, and erases every law
And all the edicts that he had ever made.
All portraits and statues he ordered to be destroyed,
No memory or record of Maximian shall remain.

"It matters not that most of the likenesses
Are linked with those of his brother Diocletian.
If the Old Man is damaged too that is his affair,
He should have been more careful of the company he kept."

So said the young Augustus and then he thought:

He did well in his time, I learnt much from him.
Without a doubt he was a singular man.
He had the authority to make men work as a team –
Proud men such as Maximian accepted his lead –
And because of this he was able to survive
And have the time to apply his active mind
To all aspects of the mechanism of state
So I can rule as the Almighty God intends.
He served his purpose; now my time has come.

— * —

DIOCLETIAN

"So it's come to this. They destroy my images.
The courier came but feared to stay to speak,
But the message was clear. No one any longer cares.

Then the other man came with the answer from the East,
They cannot or will not allow Valeria to come.
I have not the authority to save my only child.
With Galerius dead, who is to protect her now?
I answered her plea. I looked forward to having her.
My letters ignored, I had to ask others for help,
To no avail. I cannot save my child.
I am absolutely powerless. What is the point
Of living in this beautiful palace completely alone?"

— * —

Why?   Oh why?   Oh why?

A is for Aper. Aper the boar.

The sword is held on high, all watch and wait.
The sword descends, Diocles is splattered with blood,
The roar of the army throbbed in the old man's ears.

The Almighty God moves in a mysterious way.
Jupiter turned in the heavens. Indeed. Indeed.

The former Senior Augustus was laid to rest
In his mausoleum at Salona; the frieze was complete.

Sources and References

Very little is known about the career of Diocletian before he seized power on 20 November AD 284 so much of the story up to that point is conjecture. In contrast during his reign his movements can be deduced accurately from the documentation of the legal decisions which he gave. This is beautifully laid out in *Barnes: The New Empire of Diocletian and Constantine*. Diocletian was born on 22 December between 243 and 245 and again Barnes gives the sources. I have taken the earliest of these which makes him just about to be 41 when he became Emperor.

The question which has to be answered then is why did his colleagues choose him and what was his experience and what were his qualifications for the job. Of the Emperors who had held power during his adult years Aurelian was the dominant figure and must have influenced Diocletian's views on imperial governance. The campaign against Zenobia and Aurelian's life are recorded in *Zosimus: Historia Nova* and in the *Scriptores Historiae Augustae*. This latter was written in Diocletian's time and is a summary history of the all the Emperors since Hadrian. There are passing references in it to Diocletian himself including the prophesy of the druidess in Gaul and his subsequent enthusiam for hunting boars.

The great persecution is recorded in all its detail in *Lactantius: De Mortibus Persecutorum*. Lactantius was a Christian who had served at the court and was in Nicomedia at the time. The discussion between Diocletian and Galerius about the succession follows Lactantius closely. The Christians kept a written record of the acts and the last words of their martyrs and some of them have survived in *Musurillo: The Acts of the Christian Martyrs*. The trial of Maximillian is based on this but that of Bishop Anthimus is not strictly his and follows another from the collection. There was a letter written to Antioch by Lucian about his martyrdom and only the opening greeting survives which has been included as the second stanza of the poem.

Diocletian's Palace at Salona partly survives in the old town in Split. There were ancient Egyptian pillars and sphinxes incorporated in the design. *Skeat: Papyri from Panapolis* contains part of the letter books of the district officers at Panapolis on the Nile in lower Egypt in 298 to 300. These detail the daily routine and include a reference to the need for additional ships to transport the remaining columns down river before the water level falls together with the receipt forms to to be used "so that the zeal of each one of you for the divine command may be more clearly manifested". Were these columns destined for the palace at Salona?

SOURCES and REFERENCES

Cornell & Matthews: Atlas of the Roman World is a magnificent source for those wanting to visualise the story on the ground and there are the historic listings of itineraries including the resthouses in the *Itinerarium Burdigalensis*.

A short cut to many of the original references is contained in *Dodgeon & Lieu: The Roman Eastern Frontier and the Persian Wars AD 226–363* which includes the speech by Apharban which so nearly derailed the peace negotiations in 299.

Still the most exciting overview of the period is *Gibbon: The Decline and Fall of the Roman Empire*. That is where I first discovered this singular man. The Everyman Edition has the footnotes which lead to the sources behind Gibbon's magnificent prose. *Jones: The Later Roman Empire 284–602* is the essential modern source with the army's order of battle in the *Notitia Dignitatum* in the appendices. Finally *Williams: Diocletian and the Roman Recovery* is the scholarly study of the great man which I would have liked to have written if I had not followed my impulse to do it in verse.

T. D. Barnes: *The New Empire of Diocletian and Constantine.*
    Harvard University Press. 1982

P. Brown: *The World of Late Antiquity.* Thames & Hudson. 1971

Cambridge Ancient History. Volume XII. Cambridge University Press. 1939

J. Carcopino: *Daily Life in Ancient Rome.* Penguin. 1941

T. Cornell & J. Matthews: *Atlas of the Roman World.* Facts on File. 1982

M. H. Dodgeon & S. N. C. Lieu: *The Roman Eastern Frontier and the Persian Wars. AD 226–363. A Documentary History.* Routledge. 1991

T. Frank: *An Economic History of Ancient Rome. Volume V. Appendix: The Edict of Diocletian on Maximum Prices.* John Hopkins. 1940

Edward Gibbon: *The Decline and Fall of the Roman Empire.* Chapters X – XVIII.

A. H. M. Jones: *The Later Roman Empire. 284–602.* Blackwell. 1964

Lactantius: *De Mortibus Persecutorum.* Edited by J. L. Creed.
    Oxford University Press. 1984

E. Luttwak: *The Grand Strategy of the Roman Empire. From the First Century AD to the Third.* John Hopkins. 1976

H. Musurillo: *The Acts of the Christian Martyrs.* Oxford University Press. 1972

Scriptores Historiae Augustae. Loeb Classical Library.
    Harvard University Press. 1921

H. D. Skeat: *Papyri from Panapolis 298–300.* Hodges Figgis. 1964

Vegetius: *Epitome of Military Science.* Translated Texts for Historians. Vol 16.
    Liverpool University Press. 1993

G. R. Watson: *The Roman Soldier.* Thames & Hudson. 1969

G. Webster: *The Roman Imperial Army.* Black. 1969

S. Williams: *Diocletian and the Roman Recovery.* Batsford. 1985

Imperator Caesar

Gaius Aurelius Valerius Diocletianus

Pius Felix Invictus Augustus

Pontifex Maximus

Germanicus Maximus VI

Sarmaticus Maximus IV

Persicus Maximus II

Britannicus Maximus

Carpicus Maximus

Armenicus Maximus

Medicus Maximus

Adiabenicus Maximus

Tribunica Potestate XXI

Consul X

Imperator XXI

Pater Patriae

Proconsul